POSTCARDS 1

SECOND EDITION

Greetings from Miami!

Brian Abbs • Chris Barker • Ingrid Freebairn

with **JJ Wilson and Stella Reilly**

PEARSON
Longman

Postcards 1, Second Edition

Authorized adaptation from the United Kingdom edition, entitled *Snapshot*, first edition, published by Pearson Education Limited publishing under its Longman imprint. Copyright © 1998.

American English adaptation, published by Pearson Education, Inc. Copyright © 2008.

Pearson Education, 10 Bank Street, White Plains, NY 10606

Staff credits: The people who made up the **Postcards 1, Second Edition** team, representing editorial, production, design, and manufacturing, are Sarah Bupp, Aerin Csigay, Dave Dickey, Nancy Flaggman, Ann France, Charles Green, Mike Kemper, Sasha Kintzler, Dana Klinek, Ed Lamprich, Melissa Leyva, Michael Mone, Sherri Pemberton, Liza Pleva, and Stella Reilly.
Cover design: Ann France
Text design: Ann France
Text composition: TSI Graphics
Text font: 11/14 palatino

ISBN-13: 978-0-13-815043-3
ISBN-10: 0-13-815043-5

1 2 3 4 5 6 7 8 9 10–QWD–13 12 11 10 09

Contents

Scope and Sequence

Unit	Title	Communication	Grammar
Pages 2–5	**Let's get started.**		
1 Pages 6–13	**What's your name?**	Ask about favorites Introduce yourself	Simple present of *be: am/is/are* – Affirmative statements – Negative statements Subject pronouns Questions with *be* – Yes/No questions – Information questions: *What? How old? Who?*
2 Pages 14–20	**This is Brian.**	Introduce people Ask where people and things are: *Where is? Where are?*	Prepositions of place: *in, on, above, under, at, behind, in front of* Possessive adjectives: *my, your, his, her, our, your, their*
Page 21	**Progress check Units 1 and 2 Test-taking tip:** Familiarize yourself with the entire test.		
Page 22 Page 23	**Game 1: Pack it up!** **Project 1: A snapshot of me**		
3 Pages 24–31	**Where are you from?**	Talk about where people are from Ask for and give personal information	Nouns: Singular and plural forms *This/that; these/those* Articles: *a* and *an*
Pages 32–33	**Wide Angle 1: From one country to another . . .**		
4 Pages 34–40	**Can you repeat that, please?**	Ask about birthdays Ask questions: *When? What time? What day?*	*Can* for requests Question words: *When, What time, What day +* (*am/is/are*) Prepositions of time: *in* + month, *on* + day, *at* + time
Page 41	**Progress check Units 3 and 4 Test-taking tip:** Budget your time.		
5 Pages 42–49	**I have two sisters.**	Talk about your family Describe people	Possessive forms of nouns Simple present of *have; any* – Affirmative and negative statements – Yes/No questions Information questions with *How many*
Page 50 Page 51	**Game 2: Spelling bee** **Project 2: A snapshot of someone I like**		
6 Pages 52–58	**I'm not crazy about hip-hop.**	Talk about likes and dislikes	Simple present of *like* – Affirmative and negative statements – Yes/No questions – Information questions Object pronouns: *me, you, him, her, it, us, you, them*
Page 59	**Progress check Units 5 and 6 Test-taking tip:** Ask for help and clarification.		
Pages 60–61	**Wide Angle 2: Potter teens**		

Vocabulary	Skills	Learn to learn	Pronunciation
Cardinal numbers: 21–100	*Reading:* Read information in a profile; Predict missing lines *Listening:* Listen for specific information in an interview *Speaking:* Talk about your favorites; Present your personal profile *Writing:* Write a personal profile	Familiarize yourself with English	Number stress
Things for teens	*Reading:* Match paragraphs with pictures *Listening:* Listen for specific information *Speaking:* Introduce people; Talk about where people or things are; Talk about your family *Writing:* Write about your family	Work with a learning partner	Linking sounds
Countries and nationalities	*Reading:* Read an e-mail for important information *Listening:* Listen for specific information *Speaking:* Ask questions to get personal information *Writing:* Write personal information; Write an e-mail	Know some questions in English by heart	The voiced *th* sound in *this* and *that*
Ordinal numbers	*Reading*: Read a schedule *Listening*: Listen for information about events *Speaking*: Ask for personal information; Ask about birthdays; Talk about favorite TV shows *Writing*: Fill out a personal information form; Write a schedule	Ask for help	Intonation patterns in information questions
Family members Adjectives for physical description	*Reading:* Read a family tree *Listening:* Identify people based on description *Speaking:* Ask and answer questions about family and physical description *Writing:* Write about a favorite person	Group new vocabulary into categories	Rising intonation in *Yes/No* questions
Ways of expressing likes and dislikes	*Reading:* Recognize true and false statements *Listening:* Listen for details in an interview *Speaking:* Talk about likes and dislikes; Ask and answer interview questions *Writing:* Write *Yes/No* questions with *like*	Skim for the main idea	The sound /z/

Scope and Sequence

Unit	Title	Communication	Grammar
7 Pages 62–69	**Can you count?**	Ask for permission Talk about abilities (*Can I?*)	Imperatives *Can* to talk about abilities
8 Pages 70–76	**I always get up at six-thirty.**	Talk about daily routines	Sequence words: *first, then, after that, next, finally* Adverbs of frequency: *always, usually, often, sometimes, rarely/seldom, never* *How often?* Positions of frequency adverbs
Page 77	**Progress check Units 7 and 8** **Test-taking tip:** Do easier test items first.		
Page 78 Page 79	**Game 3: Racetrack** **Project 3: A snapshot of a classmate**		
9 Pages 80–87	**Miami—A great place to be!**	Make suggestions Ask and say where places are Talk about leisure activities	Prepositions of location: *across from, in front of, behind, between, next to, on the corner of, in, on* *There is/There are* *Some* and *any*
Pages 88–89	**Wide Angle 3: Teens in Iceland: Hot pots and midnight sun**		
10 Pages 90–96	**What's Brian doing?**	Ask what someone's doing now Describe what's happening right now Talk about a house	Present continuous: *be* (*am/is/are*) + verb *-ing* – Affirmative and negative statements – *Yes/No* questions – Information questions
Page 97	**Progress check Units 9 and 10** **Test-taking tip:** Work carefully.		
11 Pages 98–105	**Did he call her again today?**	Talk about past events Express approval and disapproval	Simple past of regular verbs – Affirmative and negative statements – *Yes/No* questions – Information questions
Page 106 Page 107	**Game 4: Add up the questions** **Project 4: A snapshot of a field trip**		
12 Pages 108–114	**I really had a great time.**	Talk about the past Greet people and say good-bye Talk about occupations	Simple past of *be* (*was/were*) – Affirmative and negative statements – *Yes/No* questions – Information questions Simple past of irregular verbs – Affirmative and negative statements – *Yes/No* questions – Information questions
Page 115	**Progress check Units 11 and 12** **Test-taking tip:** Review your answers.		
Pages 116–117	**Wide Angle 4: Working teens**		

Vocabulary	Skills	Learn to learn	Pronunciation
Clock times	*Reading:* Predict missing lines *Listening:* Listen for specific information *Speaking:* Talk about abilities and talents; Ask permission to borrow something *Writing:* Write commands	Have a *can-do* attitude	The /æ/ sound in *can* and *can't*
Daily routines	*Reading:* Read for specific information; Study a graph *Listening:* Listen for specific information and complete a chart *Speaking:* Talk about routines and activities *Writing:* Write about your typical day or week	Plan your weekly and daily activities	The pronunciation of *-s* and *-es* (simple present, third person)
Places in a town or city Leisure activities	*Reading:* Read for specific information; Read a map *Listening:* Listen for specific information *Speaking:* Talk about favorite places; Make suggestions *Writing:* Organize information in a chart	Prepare before a presentation	Intonation in *Yes/No* questions and short answers
Rooms and parts of a house	*Reading:* Preview and predict an article *Listening:* Listen to an interview for specific information *Speaking:* Talk about favorite places in a house; Ask *Yes/No* questions about a picture; Ask what someone's doing now *Writing:* Write messages about weekend plans	Know how to scan an article	Stress on important words
Past time expressions Emoticons and acronyms	*Reading:* Interpret emoticons and acronyms *Listening:* Listen for specific information *Speaking:* Talk about jealousy; Ask and answer *Yes/No* questions; Talk about past events *Writing:* Write a summary using the simple past; Write information questions	Take notes in class	The pronunciation of *-d* and *-ed* (simple past)
Some occupations	*Reading:* Look up the meaning of words in an article *Listening:* Listen for specific information *Speaking:* Talk about past activities; Talk about favorite occupations *Writing:* Write a story using the simple past	Keep a list of words and expressions	The pronunciation of *was* and *were*

Joey

Brian

Annie

Liza

Andy

Robbie

Caroline

Let's get started.

Vocabulary

1 Numbers 1–20

A. (A2) **Listen and repeat the numbers.**

1 one	8 eight	15 fifteen
2 two	9 nine	16 sixteen
3 three	10 ten	17 seventeen
4 four	11 eleven	18 eighteen
5 five	12 twelve	19 nineteen
6 six	13 thirteen	20 twenty
7 seven	14 fourteen	

B. PAIRS. Close your book. Take turns counting up to 20.
A: One.
B: Two.
A: Three.

2 The English alphabet

A. (A3) **Listen and repeat the alphabet.**

Aa Bb Cc Dd Ee Ff Gg Hh Ii

Jj Kk Ll Mm Nn Oo Pp Qq Rr

Ss Tt Uu Vv Ww Xx Yy Zz

B. PAIRS. The English alphabet has five vowels. Write the vowels in the blanks.
_____ _____ _____ _____ _____

C. How many consonants are there? _____

3 Months of the year

A. (A4) **Listen and repeat the twelve months that make up a year.**

January	February	March	April
May	June	July	August
September	October	November	December

B. Write the month of each holiday or event.

1. Halloween ___October___
2. Valentine's Day _____
3. Christmas _____
4. New Year's Day _____
5. Your birthday _____

4 Days of the week

A. (A5) **Listen and repeat the days of the week.**

**Sunday   Monday   Tuesday   Wednesday
Thursday   Friday   Saturday**

B. A week has five weekdays and a two-day weekend. Look at the calendar and circle the days that make up a weekend.

JANUARY

Sunday	Monday	Tuesday	Wednesday	Thursday	Friday	Saturday
		1	2	3	4	5
6	7	8	9	10	11	12
13	14	15	16	17	18	19
20	21	22	23	24	25	26
27	28	29	30	31		

5 Colors

A. Look at the colors.

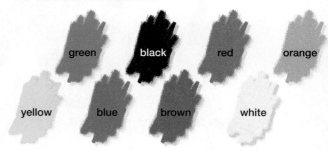

green   black   red   orange

yellow   blue   brown   white

B. PAIRS. What colors do you like? Tell your classmate.

A: I like yellow and blue.   B: I like red.

6 A classroom

A. **Look at the picture and read the labels.**

B. **PAIRS. Take turns. Ask for the colors of these things in your classroom.**

board   door   wall   desk

For example:

A: What color is the board?   **B:** Black.

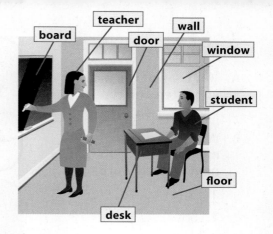

7 Classroom objects

A. **(A6) Look at the pictures as you listen and repeat the words.**

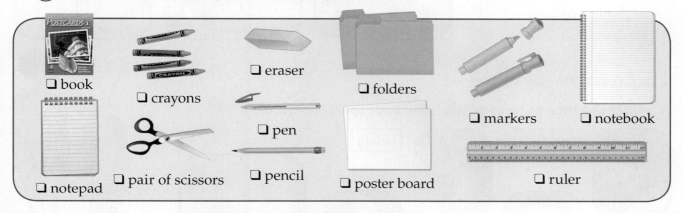

❏ book
❏ crayons
❏ eraser
❏ folders
❏ markers
❏ notebook
❏ notepad
❏ pair of scissors
❏ pen
❏ pencil
❏ poster board
❏ ruler

B. **Look at the words in Exercise A. Check (✔) the items you have.**

8 Classroom commands

A. **Look at the pictures and read the commands.**

1 Come in.
2 Stand up.
3 Sit down.
4 Open your book.
5 Close your book.
6 Write.
7 Listen.
8 Raise your hand.
9 Exchange work with a classmate.

B. **PAIRS. Student A, give a command. Student B, do Student A's command. Switch roles.**

9 Words for people

A.

A7 Look at the pictures as you listen and repeat the words.

baby   boy   girl

B. Write the name of a member from your family next to each word.

1. baby _____

2. boy _____

3. girl _____

4. teenager _____

5. man _____

6. woman _____

teenager   man   woman

10 Common adjectives

A. **A8** Look at the pictures as you listen and repeat the words.

 beautiful

young

handsome

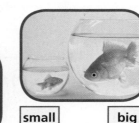

old

small   big

short   tall

B. Think of a famous person. Write three adjectives that describe that person.

Name: _____   Adjectives: _____ _____ _____

11 U.S. money

A. **A9** Listen and repeat the words.

- a penny or one cent = 1¢
- a nickel or five cents = 5¢
- a dime or ten cents = 10¢
- a quarter or twenty-five cents = 25¢

- fifty cents = 50¢
- a dollar or one dollar = $1.00
- five dollars = $5.00
- twenty dollars = $20.00

B. Write the answers.

1. five pennies = ___5¢___

2. two dimes and a nickel = _____

3. two quarters = _____

4. two nickels = _____

5. four quarters = _____

6. two ten dollars = _____

Grammar

12 Some parts of speech

A. Look at the examples of the parts of speech in the chart.

Nouns	Pronouns	Adjectives	Verbs	Prepositions	Articles
boy, girl, Australia, book	I, he, it, we, they	beautiful, small, tall	write, listen, read	from, at	a, an, the

B. PAIRS. Add two more examples in each column, except under "Articles." (Note: There are only three articles in English.)

13 Punctuation

A. Look at the punctuation.

- . (period)
- ? (question mark)
- ! (exclamation point)
- , (comma)

B. Add the correct punctuation.

A: What's your name

B: My name's Lucia

A: That's funny My name's Lucia too

Communication

14 Greetings

A10 Listen and repeat the greetings. Write the correct greeting in each balloon.

- Good morning.
- Good afternoon.
- Good evening.

1 What's your name?

1 Dialogue

A11 **Cover the dialogue and listen.**

Andy: Excuse me. Are you Brian Williams?
Brian: Yes, I am. Are you the Gibsons?
Andy: Yup. I'm Andy . . . Andy Gibson.
Liza: Hello. My name's Liza. Welcome to Miami, Brian.
Brian: Thanks! It's great to be here.
Andy: And this is my little brother.
Brian: Hi. What's your name?
Robbie: Robbie. And I'm not little. I'm six.
Brian: Nice to meet you, Robbie.
Robbie: How old are you, Brian?
Brian: I'm fifteen.
Robbie: Fifty!
Andy: No. Not fifty, Robbie. Fifteen.

2 Comprehension

A. **Look at the picture. Write the name of each person.**

B. **Write the information in the blanks.**

1. The name of the visitor _Brian Williams_

2. The names of the two brothers
   _____, _____

3. The sister's name _____

4. Brian's age _____

5. Robbie's age _____

C. **A12** **Read along as you listen again. Check your answers.**

Learning goals

Communication
Introduce yourself
Ask about favorites

Grammar
The simple present of
   be: *am/is/are*
Subject pronouns
Questions with *be*

Vocabulary
Cardinal numbers: 21–100

Brian Williams

3 Useful expressions

A. **A13** **Listen and repeat.**

- Excuse me.
- Thanks./Thank you.
- Welcome to [Miami].
- Hello. My name's [Liza].
- Are you [Brian Williams]?
- It's great to be here.

B. **Complete the conversation with expressions from Exercise A. Use your own information.**

A: ___Excuse me___. Are you _____?

B: Yes, I am.

A: _____. My name's _____.

_____.

B: _____. It's great to be here.

C. **PAIRS. Role-play the conversation in Exercise B.**

4 Vocabulary

Cardinal numbers: 21–100

A. (A14) **Listen and repeat.**

21	twenty-one
22	twenty-two
23	twenty-three
24	twenty-four
25	twenty-five
30	thirty
40	forty
50	fifty
60	sixty
70	seventy
80	eighty
90	ninety
100	one hundred

B. (A15) **Listen and circle the numbers you hear.**

22	56	(13)	55	77
10	89	95	60	15
7	20	8	30	99

5 Pronunciation

Number stress

A. (A16) **Listen to the numbers and repeat them.**

13	14	15	16
	17	18	19

30	40	50	60
	70	80	90

B. (A17) **Listen and circle the number you hear in each pair.**

1. 13 30   4. 16 60
2. 14 40   5. 17 70
3. 15 50   6. 18 80

GRAMMAR FOCUS

The simple present of *be*

Affirmative statements		Negative statements	
I **am**		I **am**	
You **are**		You **are**	
He **is**		He **is**	
She **is**	11 years old.	She **is**	not 15 years old.
It **is**		It **is**	
We **are**		We **are**	
You **are**		You **are**	
They **are**		They **are**	

Long forms	Short forms (Contractions)
I am	**I'm**
You are	**You're**
He is	**He's**
She is	**She's**
It is	**It's**
We are	**We're**
You are	**You're**
They are	**They're**

Discovering grammar

Look at the grammar chart. Complete the grammar rules.

1. The present tense of *be* has three forms: ___*am*___,
   _____, and _____.

2. Use the verb _____ with *I*.

3. Use the verb _____ with *he*, *she*, and *it*.

4. Use the verb _____ with *we*, *you*, and *they*.

Practicing grammar

6 Practice

Write the contractions (short forms).

1. (*I am*) ___*I'm*___ a student.

2. (*You are*) _____ my teacher.

3. (*She is*) _____ my friend.

4. (*He is*) _____ 10 years old.

5. (*It is*) _____ my English homework.

6. (*They are*) _____ my friends.

7. (*We are*) _____ classmates.

7 Practice

A. Label the pictures with the people's occupations. An occupation can be used more than once.

actor	movie director	talk show host
~~author~~	singer	tennis player

B. Write two sentences saying who the person in each picture is and his or her occupation.

1. _She's J.K. Rowling._
   She's an author.

2. _____
   _____

3. _____
   _____

4. _____
   _____

5. _____
   _____

6. _____
   _____

7. _____
   _____

C. PAIRS. Student A, say the names of three people in the pictures. Student B, say the person's occupation.

For example:

A: She's J.K. Rowling.
B: She's an author.

D. Switch roles. Talk about three more people in the pictures.

1. J.K. Rowling
   author

2. Chayanne
   _____

3. Gwen Stefani
   _____

4. Oprah Winfrey
   _____

5. Maria Sharapova
   _____

6. Steven Spielberg
   _____

7. Daniel Radcliffe
   _____

Unit 1

GRAMMAR FOCUS

Questions with *be*

Yes/No questions	Affirmative answers	Negative answers	
Am I	Yes, you **are**.	No, you**'re** not.	(No, you **aren't**.)
Are you	Yes, I **am**.	No, I**'m** not.	
Is he	Yes, he **is**.	No, he**'s** not.	(No, he **isn't**.)
Is she OK?	Yes, she **is**.	No, she**'s** not.	(No, she **isn't**.)
Is it	Yes, it **is**.	No, it**'s** not.	(No, it **isn't**.)
Are we	Yes, we/you **are**.	No, we**'re**/you**'re** not.	(No, we/you **aren't**.)
Are you	Yes, we **are**.	No, we**'re** not.	(No, we **aren't**.)
Are they	Yes, they **are**.	No, they**'re** not.	(No, they **aren't**.)

Information questions	Long answers	Short answers
What's your name?	My name's Isabel.	Isabel.
How old are you?	I'm 10 years old.	Ten.
Who's your favorite singer?	My favorite singer is Shakira.	Shakira.

Contractions

What's = What is   *Who's* = Who is   *name's* = name is

Discovering grammar

Look at the grammar chart. Circle the correct answers.

1. Use the question word (*Who* / *What*) to ask a person's name.
2. Use the question word(s) (*What* / *How old*) to ask about a person's age.
3. (*What's* / *Whats'*) is the contraction of *What is*.

Practicing grammar

8 Practice

Change these sentences into *Yes/No* questions. Change the subject pronoun as needed.

1. I'm 10 years old. ___Are you 10 years old?___
2. You're my friend. _____
3. Our teacher is nice. _____
4. English is easy. _____
5. Our classmates are cool. _____
6. I'm happy. _____

9 Practice

PAIRS. Take turns. Ask each other the questions in Exercise 8. Give true answers.

For example:

A: Are you 10 years old?
B: No, I'm not. I'm 11.

10 Practice

Look at the answers. Write the question for each answer. Use a question mark.

1. **A:** ___What's your name?___
   B: Sophia. Sophia Garcia.

2. **A:** _____
   B: Christina Aguilera. She's a great singer.

3. **A:** _____
   B: I'm 12.

4. **A:** _____
   B: Yes, I'm OK.

11 Practice

Play a game! Go to page 130.

12 Communication

Ask about favorites

A. (A18) **Listen to the conversation.**

> **A:** Who's your favorite actor?
> **B:** <u>Johnny Depp</u>.
> **A:** Really? What about your favorite athlete?
> **B:** My favorite athlete is <u>Michelle Wie</u>.
> **A:** Me, too. She's great.

B. **PAIRS.** **Role-play the conversation. Use your own information.**

GROUPS. **Talk about your favorite singers and actors.**

Useful language:
- Who's/What's your favorite _____?
- He's/She's really cool!
- Me, too!
- He's/She's my favorite, too.
- Really?
- Yeah.

13 Listening

A. (A19) **Listen to the interviews. Who are the teenagers' favorite athletes? Put a check (✔) before the names.**

_____ Michael Jordan
_____ Romario
_____ Shaquille O'Neal
_____ Ronaldo
_____ Diego Maradona
✔ Jorge Campos

B. **Put a check (✔) before the names of the two teenagers in the interviews.**

_____ Luis Cesar Chavez
_____ Igor Gonzales
_____ Luis Diego Chavez
_____ Gustavo Senna

C. **Put a check (✔) before the name of the radio program.**

_____ "Teen Fun"
_____ "Teen Line"
_____ "Teen Show"

Learn to learn

Familiarize yourself with English.
Listening to English often will help you become familiar with the sounds of English.

(A20) Listen again to the interview. Listen a few times if necessary. Then answer the questions.

1. What's the name of the host of the radio program?
   _____ *David* _____

2. What's the question for the week?
   _____

3. What's the name of the interviewer in Mexico? _____

4. What's the name of the interviewer in Brazil? _____

Tip: Whenever you can, watch TV shows in English or listen to songs in English.

14 Reading

A21 **Read the profiles of teenagers looking for e-friends. Then listen to their messages.**

E-FRIENDS WANTED

Name: Jiang Li
City/Town: Shunde
State/Province: Guangdong
Country: China
Message:

Hi. My name's Jiang Li. I'm 13 years old, and I'm in sixth grade. I like movies and music. My favorite actress is Zhang Ziyi.

Name: John
City/Town: Bedford
State/Province: Connecticut
Country: U.S.A.
Message:

Hi there. I'm John, and I'm 12 years old. I like texting friends. I also like movies and sports. I love the *Star Wars* movies!

Name: Mia
City/Town: Treviso
Country: Italy
Message:

My name's Mia. I'm 14. I speak English, Spanish, and Italian. I love all the Harry Potter books and movies.

15 Comprehension

Complete the chart.

	Jiang Li	John	Mia
Age			
City/ State/ Country			
Favorites			

16 Writing

A. Create your own profile.

Name: _____
Age: _____
School: _____
City/Town: _____
Country: _____
Favorites: _____
_____

B. **CLASS.** **Present your profile to the class.**

For example:

Hello. My name's Antonio. I'm 11 years old. I'm from Madrid, Spain. My favorite sport is volleyball.

Putting it together   *At the airport*

A. Before you listen, read the conversation. Fill in the missing questions.

So, what grade are you in, Liza?

I'm in eighth grade. Andy's in ninth.

1

Really? (1) _____?

I'm 14.

Yeah, she's old.

2

No, Robbie. Liza's not old. Hey, look what I have for you.

A koala bear! Thanks! (2) _____?

3

His name? Umm. Aussie. Yeah, his name's Aussie.

Cool!

(3) _____?

4

My favorite singer? Well, I like the band U2. Who's your favorite?

Me? Ashlee Simpson.

Eww! Ashlee Simpson! Yuck! She can't sing.

5

So, Liza, do you like Brian?

6

B. **A22** Now listen as you read along. Check your answers.

2 This is Brian.

1 Dialogue

(A23) **Cover the dialogue and listen.**

Robbie: There's my mom.

Brian: Where's your dad?

Liza: He's at work.

Robbie: No, he's not. He's at home today.

Andy: Yeah, Dad's at home. Mom, this is Brian.

Mom: Hello, Brian. Nice to meet you. How are you?

Brian: I'm OK, thanks. Just a little tired.

Mom: Where are your bags?

Brian: They're on the cart over there.

Mom: Andy, please put Brian's bags in the car.

Robbie: Let's go, Mom.

(Later, at home.)

Robbie: Come on, Brian. I'll show you my room and my new video games.

Liza: Robbie, Brian's tired. Leave him alone. OK?

2 Comprehension

A. Match the two parts to make sentences.

1. Mom is
2. Dad is
3. Brian is
4. The bags are
5. Andy puts the bags

a. on the cart.
b. tired.
c. at the airport.
d. in the car.
e. at home.

B. **(A24)** **Read along as you listen again. Check your answers.**

Learning goals

Communication
Introduce people
Ask where people and things are:
Where is?/Where are?

Grammar
Prepositions of place: *in, on, above, under, at, behind, in front of*
Possessive adjectives

Vocabulary
Things for teens

3 Useful expressions

A. (A25) **Listen and repeat.**

- Come on.
- I'm OK, thanks. / Fine, thanks.
- Nice to meet you.
- How are you?

B. **Write the appropriate responses. Use the expressions from Exercise A.**

1. **A:** How are you?

   B: _____

2. **A:** _____

   B: Nice to meet you, too.

3. **A:** _____

   B: OK. Let's go.

4 Communication

Introduce people

A. (A26) **Listen to the conversation.**

   A: <u>Mrs. Salas</u>, this is <u>Monica</u>.
   B: Nice to meet you, <u>Monica</u>. How are you?
   C: Fine, thanks.

B. **GROUPS.** **Write a conversation introducing a friend to your mom or dad. Use Exercise A as a model.**

   A: _____

   B: _____

   C: _____

C. **GROUPS.** **Role-play the conservation.**

5 Pronunciation

Linking sounds

A. (A27) **Listen. Then listen again and repeat.**

- Where's your dad?
- He's at work.
- He's at home.
- This is Brian.
- Nice to meet you.
- How are you?

B. **PAIRS. Practice the conversations with a classmate.**

1. **A:** Where's your dad?
   B: He's at home.
2. **A:** This is Sara.
   B: Nice to meet you.

6 Vocabulary

Things for teens

A. (A28) **Look at the pictures as you listen and repeat.**

1. cell phone _____
2. skateboard _____
3. MP3 player _____
4. computer _____

5. DVDs _____
6. DVD player _____
7. video games _____
8. television _____

9. magazines _____
10. backpack _____
11. bicycle _____
12. Rollerblades® _____

B. **Look at the words in Exercise A. Put a check (✔) next to the things you have.**

GRAMMAR FOCUS

Prepositions of place: *in, on, above, under, at, behind, in front of*

Where are the CDs?
They're **in** the bag.
They're **on** the bag.

Where's the balloon?
It's **above** the table.
It's **in front of** the TV.

Where's the balloon?
It's **under** the table.
It's **behind** the computer.

Where's your sister?
She's **at** work.
She's **at** home.
She's **at** school.

Discovering grammar

Look at the grammar chart. Circle the correct answers.

1. What are some examples of prepositions?
   - **a.** the
   - **b.** at
   - **c.** under
   - **d.** an
   - **e.** in front of
   - **f.** in

2. What usually comes after a preposition?
   - **a.** a verb
   - **b.** a noun
   - **c.** an adjective

Practicing grammar

7 Practice

PAIRS. Take turns asking and answering the questions.

1. Where's our teacher?
   She's in front of the class.
2. Where's your English book?
3. Where's your backpack?
4. Where are your pens and pencils?
5. Where are your notebooks?

8 Practice

A. PAIRS. Compete with another pair. Look at the picture. In three minutes, write sentences that say where the objects are. Use prepositions.

For example:

The video camera is above the bed.

_____

_____

_____

_____

B. Count your sentences. Who has the most sentences?

9 Practice

Have a competition! Go to page 130.

10 Listening

A. (A29) Listen to the conversation. Circle the correct answers.

1. Where's the family?
   - **a.** at the park
   - **(b.)** at home
2. Where's Liza?
   - **a.** at the computer
   - **b.** on the phone
3. Where are Andy and Brian?
   - **a.** in the bedroom
   - **b.** at school
4. Where's Robbie?
   - **a.** in the bedroom
   - **b.** in the kitchen
5. Where's dinner?
   - **a.** in the bag
   - **b.** on the table

B. (A30) Listen again and check your work.

GRAMMAR FOCUS

Possessive adjectives

Subject pronouns	Possessive adjectives	Sentences
I	my	**My** name is Brian.
you	your	**Your** name is Robbie.
he	his	**His** name is Andy.
she	her	**Her** name is Liza.
we	our	**Our** last name is Gibson.
you	your	**Your** names are Robbie, Andy, and Liza.
they	their	**Their** last name is Cordova.

Discovering grammar

Look at the grammar chart. Circle the correct answers.

1. What are some examples of possessive adjectives?
   - **a.** we
   - **b.** your
   - **c.** they
   - **d.** their
   - **e.** his
   - **f.** our

2. What comes after a possessive adjective?
   - **a.** a verb
   - **b.** a noun
   - **c.** a pronoun

Practicing grammar

11 Practice

Complete the sentences with the correct possessive adjectives.

1. _My_ English book is fun. (*I*)
2. We love ____ teachers. (*we*)
3. ____ cell phone looks really cool. (*You*)
4. ____ parents are nice. (*They*)
5. ____ name is Brad. (*He*)
6. I like ____ new hairstyle. (*she*)

Paste your photo here.

12 Practice

Paste your photo in the space provided. Then complete the sentences with possessive adjectives.

1. _Her_ name is Liza.
2. ____ name is Andy.
3. ____ name is Robbie.
4. ____ last name is Gibson.
5. ____ name is Caroline.
6. ____ boyfriend is Andy.
7. ____ name is ____.
   (Write your name.)
8. ____ last name is ____.
   (Write your last name.)

13 Practice

A. Circle the correct answers.

Robbie: Brian, can I show you (**1.** *my* / *her*) room?

Brian: Sure. Where is (**2.** *my* / *your*) room?

Robbie: Here it is. And here's (**3.** *his* / *my*) favorite baseball. It's from my best friend.

Brian: Cool. Let's play baseball later. So, where are the other rooms?

Robbie: This is Liza's room. See those posters in her room? That poster is (**4.** *their* / *her*) favorite.

Brian: Yeah, that's a nice poster! How about Andy's room?

Robbie: It's that one. (**5.** *His* / *Her*) room is big. I can't go into (**6.** *his* / *her*) room. He always says, "Knock first." (**7.** *My* / *His*) computer's in there. I can't use it. I think that's (**8.** *your* / *my*) room, too, Brian.

Brian: And where's (**9.** *my* / *your*) parents' room?

Robbie: See that big door? That's (**10.** *her* / *their*) room. We can't go in there.

Brian: That's OK. Come on. Let's bring (**11.** *their* / *my*) bags up.

B. (A31) **Listen and check your answers.**

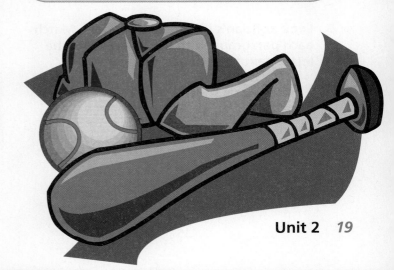

A

B

C

D

14 Reading

A. (A32) **Read along silently as you listen.**

1. *This is my mother. Her name's Lucille. And that's my father. His name's George. They're at home in Canberra.* ___B___

2. *This is my little sister. Her name's Sandra, Sandy for short. She's 13. Here she is at school.* _____

3. *This is my big sister, Louise. She's eighteen years old. She's a ballet student. Here she is in her ballet class.* _____

4. *This is my dog, Tigger. He's in the backyard.* _____

B. Look at Brian's pictures from home. Match each paragraph with a picture. Write the letter next to each paragraph.

C. PAIRS. Write a quiz.

- Write three information questions about Brian's family.

- Give your questions to a classmate.
- Write the answers to your classmate's questions.
- Check your classmate's answers. Who answered all the questions correctly?

PAIRS. Talk about your family.

Useful language:
- What's your dad's/mom's name?
- How old is/are _____?
- Really?
- Where's _____?
- He's/She's _____.

15 Writing

Complete the paragraph with *is*, *am*, or *are* and your information. Try to add two more sentences.

My mom's name ____*is*____ _____. She _____ _____. My dad's name _____ _____. He _____ _____. They _____ _____.

Progress check Units 1 and 2

Test-taking tip: Familiarize yourself with the test.
When you receive your test, quickly read the directions and a few items. Make sure you know what to do.

Grammar

A. Write the contractions. (1 point each)

1. (*I am*) _____I'm_____ great!
2. (*You are*) _____ cool.
3. (*They are*) _____ nice.
4. (*He is*) _____ OK.
5. (*She is*) _____ good.
6. (*We are*) _____ fine.
7. (*It is*) _____ fun.

B. Give true answers. (2 points each)

1. Are you nine years old? _No, I'm not. I'm 10._
2. Are you in fifth grade? _____
3. Is your mother a teacher? _____
4. Are your classmates all girls?

   _____
5. Is English easy? _____
6. Are you and your friends 15?

   _____

C. Complete the sentences with possessive adjectives. (1 point each)

1. That's _____my_____ dad. I love him.
2. She's my mom. _____ name's Kim.
3. These are my dogs. _____ names are Puff and Magic.
4. He's my brother. _____ name is Tim.
5. She's _____ teacher. We like her.

D. Circle the correct answers. (1 point each)

1. My books are (*at* / (*in*)) my backpack.
2. The computer is (*on* / *in*) the table.
3. The board is (*behind* / *at*) the desk.
4. My backpack is (*in* / *under*) my chair.
5. The clock is (*above* / *in*) the board.
6. I am (*at* / *on*) school right now.

Vocabulary

E. Write the numbers in words. (1 point each)

1. 20 _____twenty_____
2. 86 _____
3. 90 _____
4. 62 _____
5. 47 _____
6. 35 _____

F. Fill in the missing letters to complete the words for things for teens. (1 point each)

Things for teens	
s k _a_ _t_ _e_ _b_ _o_ _a_ r d	_ a _ k p _ _ _ k
c e _ _ _ p h _ _ _ _	c _ _ p _ t e _
b i _ _ _ _ l e	t _ _ _ _ v _ s i _ _ _

Communication

G. Complete the conversations. Use your own information. (2 points each sentence)

1. A: _____What's your name_____?
   B: My name's _____.
2. A: _____?
   B: I'm _____ years old.
3. A: _____?
   B: I'm fine, thanks.
4. A: _____?
   B: My favorite actor is _____.
5. A: Where are you right now?
   B: _____.

> **Now I can . . .**
> ❏ introduce myself and others.
> ❏ talk about personal information.
> ❏ say where people and things are.

Game 1 *Pack it up!*

Steps:

1. Work in teams of five or six.

2. Look at the picture. Try to memorize the location of each item.

3. Your teacher will draw a "box" on the board for each team.

4. Close your books. Player A from each team stands up.

5. The teacher asks a *Where* question about one of the items on the page—for example: *Where are the books?* The first standing player who raises his or her hand can answer the question. If the answer is correct, the teacher writes the name of the item in the team's box. If the answer is incorrect, the teacher gives the other teams another chance. Then the game begins again with Player B on each team.

6. The team with the most items wins!

Useful language

- Way to go!
- Excellent!
- Ah, too bad…

Project 1   *A snapshot of me*

Make a scrapbook. Write a paragraph about yourself and your interests on each page. Find a photograph or illustration for each paragraph. Use Madison's scrapbook below as a guide. Show and read your scrapbook to your group or class.

1. Introduce yourself.

Hi! My name is Madison Jones. I'm 12 years old. This is a picture of me and my cat. My cat's name is Henry.

I live in Aliso Viejo, California. It's near Los Angeles. It's a beautiful city and there's a lot to do. I really like it.

2. Write about where you live.

3. Write about your school and your classes.

I'm in the seventh grade at Aliso Viejo Middle School. My favorite subjects are math and gym. I don't like history. It's boring.

My favorite sport is soccer. My favorite soccer player is Ronaldinho. He's Brazilian. He's a fabulous player.

4. Write about your favorite singer, athlete, movie star, or TV star.

3 Where are you from?

1 Vocabulary

Countries and nationalities

A. **Look at the map. Label your country and Australia.**

B. **Fill in the missing countries and nationalities in the chart below.**

C. (A33) **Listen and check your answers.**

2 Communication

Talk about where people are from

A. (A34) **Listen to the conversation.**

 A: Is <u>J.K. Rowling</u> American?
 B: No, <u>she's</u> not.
 A: Where's <u>she</u> from?
 B: <u>She's from Great Britain</u>.
 A: What's <u>her</u> nationality?
 B: <u>She's British</u>.

B. **PAIRS. Role-play the conversation. Replace "J.K. Rowling" with another famous person.**

Countries	Nationalities
Australia	Australi**an**
Brazil	Brazili**an**
Canada	_____
Colombia	Colombi**an**
_____	Costa Ric**an**
Korea	_____
Mexico	Mexic**an**
_____	Morocc**an**
United States	_____
_____	Venezuel**an**
Finland	Finn**ish**
Great Britain	Brit**ish**
Poland	_____
China	Chin**ese**
Japan	_____
_____	Leban**ese**

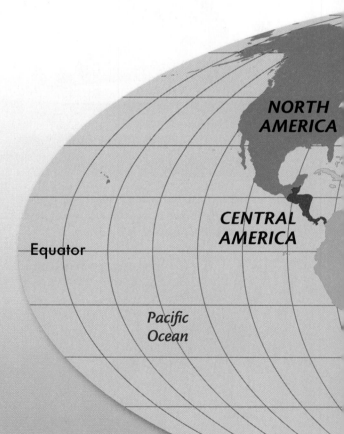

NORTH
AMERICA

CENTRAL
AMERICA

Equator

Pacific
Ocean

TEEN TALK

PAIRS. Ask where these famous people are from and what their nationalities are:

- Daniel Radcliffe
- Anna Kournikova
- Ichiro Suzuki
- Charlize Theron

Useful language:
- Where's _____ from?
- He's/She's from _____.
- What's his/her nationality?
- He's/She's _____.
- Really?
- She is?
- What about _____?

Learn to learn

Learn some questions in English by heart.

It is helpful to learn a few questions in English to ask when you meet people.

PAIRS/GROUPS. Go over Units 1–3. List four more useful questions you should know by heart.

What's your name?

How are you?

_____

_____

_____

_____

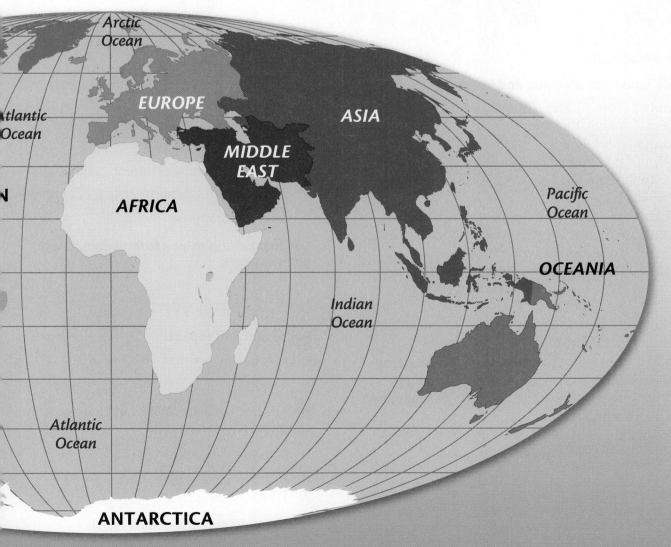

Arctic Ocean

EUROPE

ASIA

MIDDLE EAST

Atlantic Ocean

AFRICA

Pacific Ocean

OCEANIA

Indian Ocean

Atlantic Ocean

ANTARCTICA

3 Dialogue

A35 **Cover the dialogue and listen.**

Andy: Hey, look out!

Eric: Oops. I'm sorry!

Andy: It's OK.

Eric: Are you all right?

Andy: Yeah, I'm fine. Eric! It's you!

Eric: Hi, guys.

Liza: Hi, Eric. Those skates are really cool.

Eric: Thanks. They're great for tricks. Want to see a cool trick?

Liza: Nah, not right now, maybe later. Uh, Eric, this is Brian. He's an exchange student. Brian, Eric.

Eric: Nice to meet you, Brian. Where are you from?

Brian: I'm from Australia, from Canberra.

Eric: So you're Australian. Awesome! . . . Excuse me . . . I have to go. See you in school, Brian.

Brian: Bye.

4 Comprehension

A. **Answer *True* or *False*. Circle the wrong information in the false statements.**

1. Andy and Eric are friends. _____*True*_____

2. Liza likes Eric's skates. _____

3. Eric is an exchange student. _____

4. Brian is from Canberra. _____

5. Brian is American. _____

B. **A36** **Read along as you listen again. Check your answers.**

5 Useful expressions

A. **A37** **Listen and repeat.**

- Look out!
- Are you all right?
- I'm sorry!
- I'm fine.

B. **PAIRS. Use the expressions in Exercise A to complete the conversation.**

A: Hey, _____*look out!*_____

B: Oops. _____ _____

A: Yeah, _____

C. **PAIRS. Role-play the conversation.**

GRAMMAR FOCUS

NOUNS: Singular and plural forms

Singular noun (one)	Plural noun (more than one)
 book	 books

Plurals of regular nouns

Group 1: Most nouns

student → students   apple → apples   Australian → Australians

Group 2: Nouns ending in -x, -s, -z, -ch, and -sh

box → boxes   dress → dresses   lunch → lunches

Group 3: Nouns ending in a consonant + -y

city → cities   country → countries   baby → babies

Group 4: Nouns ending in a vowel + -y

boy → boys   key → keys   day → days

Plurals of irregular nouns

man → **men**   child → **children**   foot → **feet**

person → **people**   tooth → **teeth**   mouse → **mice**

Discovering grammar

Look at the grammar chart. Circle the correct answers.

To form the plurals of . . .

1. . . . most singular nouns, add (-d / -s).
2. . . . nouns ending in -x, -s, -z, -ch, and -sh, add (-es / -s).
3. . . . nouns ending in a consonant + -y, change y to i and add (-s / -es).

Practicing grammar

6 Practice

PAIRS. Take turns saying and spelling the plural forms of these nouns.

For example:

A: I'll start. Country—countries.
C-o-u-n-t-r-i-e-s. Your turn.

1. city
2. fax
3. address
4. woman
5. party
6. boy
7. sandwich
8. tree
9. actor

7 Practice

Have a competition! Go to page 130.

8 Practice

PAIRS. Take turns. Change these sentences. Use plural nouns and plural verbs.

For example:

The <u>dictionary</u> is on the teacher's desk.
The **dictionaries are** on the teacher's desk.

1. The <u>story</u> is very exciting.
2. The new <u>toy</u> is so cool.
3. The <u>child</u> is really smart.
4. My <u>class</u> is easy.
5. His <u>foot</u> is big.
6. The <u>woman</u> is very pretty.

GRAMMAR FOCUS

This/that; these/those

Singular	Plural
This is a book.	**These are** books.
That's an apple.	**Those** are apples.

Articles: *a* and *an*

Singular	Plural
He's **a** student.	They're students.
It's **an** eraser.	They're erasers.
She's **an** exchange student.	They're exchange students.

Discovering grammar

Look at the grammar chart. Circle the correct answers.

1. Use (*this* / *that*) to talk about an object or person that's near you.
2. Use (*these* / *those*) to talk about two or more objects or people that are far from you.
3. Use (*a* / *an*) before a word that begins with a vowel sound.
4. Use (*a* / *an*) before a word that begins with a consonant sound.

Practicing grammar

9 Practice

Look at the pictures. Complete the sentences with *this*, *that*, *these*, or *those*.

1. _Those_ red shoes are beautiful!
2. I like _____ blue backpack.
3. _____ jacket is expensive!
4. _____ pink cell phone is so cool.
5. Is _____ your wallet?
6. _____ umbrellas are really nice.

10 Practice

PAIRS. Compete with a classmate. Write *a* or *an* before each noun as fast as you can.

1. _a_ woman
2. ____ boy
3. ____ apple
4. ____ answer
5. ____ child
6. ____ computer
7. ____ old man
8. ____ cool trick
9. ____ orange
10. ____ person
11. ____ student
12. ____ teacher
13. ____ easy test
14. ____ American
15. ____ skateboard
16. ____ television

11 Practice

Complete the responses with *a* or *an*.

1. **A:** What's that?

   B: It's _*an*_ audiocassette.

2. **A:** What's this?

   B: It's ____ DVD player.

3. **A:** What's that?

   B: It's ____ electronic pen.

4. **A:** Is that a DVD player?

   B: No, it's not. It's ____ CD player.

5. **A:** Is that a cell phone?

   B: No, it's not. It's ____ iPod®.

6. **A:** Is this ____ camera?

   B: No, it's not. It's ____ MP3 player.

12 Practice

PAIRS. Compete with another pair. Ask for the names of five objects in your classroom. Use *this*, *that*, *these*, or *those*. The first pair to finish wins.

For example:

A: What's that on the wall?

B: It's a map.

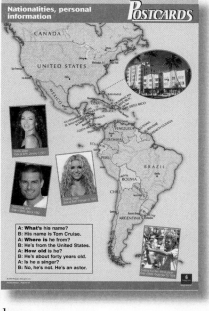

13 Pronunciation

The voiced *th* sound in _this_ and _that_

A. (A38) **Listen and repeat.**

this	that	they
these	those	there

A: What's this? A camera phone?   **B:** No, that's an MP3 player.

A: What's that?   **B:** That's an Indian dress.

A: Whose dogs are those?   **B:** Those are theirs.

A: Those skates are cool.   **B:** They're great for tricks, too.

B. (A39) **PAIRS. Listen again to the conservations in Exercise A. Practice them with a classmate.**

14 Listening

(A40) **Listen to the conversation. Then circle the correct answers.**

1. Who is the visitor?
   a. Britney   **(b.)** Ana   **c.** Mom

2. Whose bedroom is it?
   a. Britney's   **b.** Ana's   **c.** the dog's

3. Where does Britney watch TV?
   a. in her bedroom   **b.** in the living room   **c.** in the den

4. Whose bed is comfortable?
   a. Britney's   **b.** Ana's   **c.** Tiffany's

5. Who is Tiffany?
   a. Britney's sister   **b.** Britney's dog   **c.** Britney's mom

15 Reading

A. List your favorite activities. _____ _____ _____

B. (A41) Read along silently as you listen. Underline the students' favorite forms of entertainment.

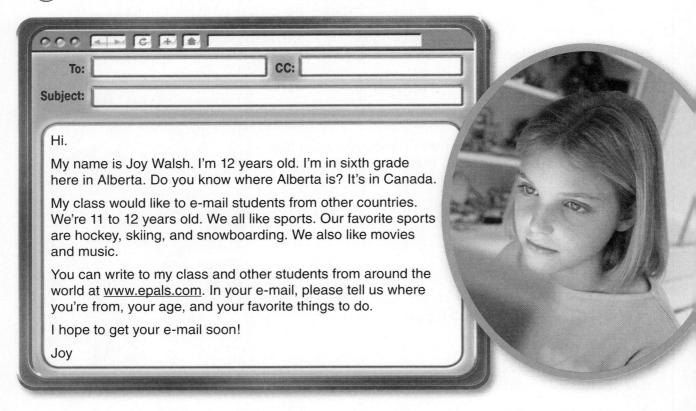

To: _____ CC: _____

Subject: _____

Hi.

My name is Joy Walsh. I'm 12 years old. I'm in sixth grade here in Alberta. Do you know where Alberta is? It's in Canada.

My class would like to e-mail students from other countries. We're 11 to 12 years old. We all like sports. Our favorite sports are hockey, skiing, and snowboarding. We also like movies and music.

You can write to my class and other students from around the world at www.epals.com. In your e-mail, please tell us where you're from, your age, and your favorite things to do.

I hope to get your e-mail soon!

Joy

C. Answer these questions.

1. What's the e-mail writer's name?
   Joy Walsh

2. Where's she from?
   _____

3. What's her nationality?
   _____

4. How old are the students in her class?
   _____

5. What are their favorite sports?
   _____

6. What website can you visit to e-mail students from around the world?
   _____

16 Your turn

GROUPS. Talk about what you would like to tell Joy and her classmates. Use these questions to guide you. Make notes in your notebook.

1. What are your names?
2. How old are you?
3. Where are you from?
4. What are your favorite activities?
5. What's your favorite book or movie?

17 Writing

A. GROUPS. Write your group e-mail using your answers to the questions in Exercise 16. Read your e-mail aloud to the class or post it on the board and have your classmates read it.

B. If your class is interested, check out http://www.epals.com with your teacher and choose a class to write to.

Putting it together   *At school*

A. Before you listen, read the conversation. Complete Annie's questions.

Hi, Annie.

Hi, Liza. Is that a happy smile? What's going on?

1

Well, he's here! He's at my house.

(1) _____ here?

The exchange student.

2

Oh? (2) _____ he?

He's 15.

3

Perfect. We're 14.

(3) _____ cute?

Totally. And those eyes—they're to die for!

4

Really? (4) _____ his name? (5) _____ he _____?

His name's Brian, and he's from Australia.

5

Can I come to your house tonight?

Um . . . no. Not tonight.

Why not?

Because.

6

B. (A42) **Now listen and check your answers. Discuss: Do you think Liza wants Annie to meet Brian? Underline the part in the conversation that supports your answer.**

1 Reading

> **Reading skill:** Reading for specific information
> When you read, look for answers to questions.

A. Quickly read about Yaching and Daniel. Where are they from? Where are they now? Circle the answers in the reading.

B. Read the article and fill in the chart for Daniel and Yaching.

	Daniel	Yaching	Mike
Nationality	*Brazilian*		
Country			
First language			
Second language			
Now lives in			
Student at			
Thinks new city is			
The people are			

Daniel Santos is Brazilian. H[...]
in the United States for a ye[...]

2 Listening

A43 Listen to a program on International Teen Web Radio. DJ Ellen Sandoval, 13, is interviewing an exchange student, Mike Smith. Complete the chart above for Mike.

3 Speaking

PAIRS. Imagine your partner lives in another country. Interview him or her using the questions below. Take notes. Then change roles.

1. *What's your first language?*
2. *Where are you from?*
3. *What's your second language?*
4. *Where are you now?*
5. *How is it?*
6. *How are the people?*

Yaching Chen is Taiwanes[...]
She's in Switzerland with [...]
her mother and father.

4 Writing

Write a paragraph about your partner. Use the notes from your interview.

From One Country to Another . . .

"Hi, I'm Daniel Santos and I'm from Brasilia, Brazil. My first language is Portuguese. My second language is English. I'm an exchange student at a high school in Santa Fe, New Mexico. All my classes are in English. I really like Santa Fe. It's cool. The people here are very relaxed and friendly. The weather is great. And the adobe buildings are awesome."

"Hello. My name's Yaching Chen. Taiwanese is my first language, and English is my second language. I'm from Taipei, Taiwan. But now I live in Geneva, Switzerland. My father works here. Geneva is very international, and Lake Geneva is beautiful. The people here are really interesting. They speak a lot of different languages—French, German, Italian—and most people also speak English. I'm in an international school, and all our classes are in English."

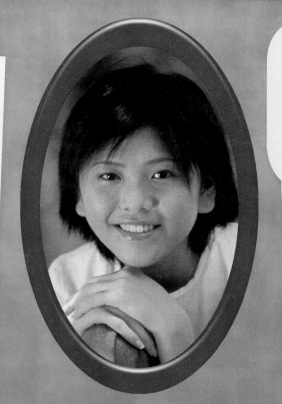

4 Can you repeat that, please?

1 Dialogue

A44 Cover the dialogue and listen.

Andy: Good morning. Can I ask you a question?

Woman: Of course.

Andy: Can you give my friend a guest pass?

Woman: Sure. What's your last name?

Brian: Williams.

Woman: Can you spell that, please?

Brian: W-I-L-L-I-A-M-S.

Woman: And your first name?

Brian: Brian. B-R-I-A-N.

Woman: What's your address?

Brian: 55 Isabel Street, Coral Gables, Florida.

Andy: The zip code is 33134.

Woman: And your phone number?

Andy: (305) 555-1366.

Woman: I'm sorry. Can you repeat the last four digits, please?

Andy: 1366.

Woman: 1-3-6-6. What's your date of birth, Brian?

Brian: October 15th, 1991.

Woman: Here you go. Is there anything else?

Brian: No, that's it. Thanks!

Woman: You're welcome.

Learning goals

Communication
Ask for personal information
Ask questions: *When? What time? What day?*

Grammar
Can for requests
Question words: *When, What time, What day* + *(am/is/are)*
Prepositions of time: *in* + month; *on* + day; *at* + time

Vocabulary
Ordinal numbers

2 Comprehension

A. **Fill out Brian's guest pass.**

B. **A45** **Check your answers. Read along as you listen again.**

GUEST PASS

Last name: *Williams*

First name: _____

Date of birth: _____

Address: _____

_____

Phone number: _____

Signature: *Brian Williams*

Valid for September 21 only

3 Your turn

Fill out the form with your own information.

**RECREATION CENTER
MEMBERSHIP APPLICATION FORM**

Last name _____ First name _____ Date of birth _____

Street address _____ City/Town _____

State _____ Zip code _____ Country _____

Home phone _____ E-mail _____

Signature _____

4 Useful expressions

A. (A46) **Listen and repeat.**

- Here you go.
- Can you repeat that?
- Yes, please.
- Sure.
- No, that's it.
- Is there anything else?

B. Complete the conversation with expressions from Exercise A. Use your own information for the responses.

A: Hi. Can I get a library card?

B: ___*Sure*___. What's your name?

A: _____.

B: I'm sorry. _____?

A: _____. _____.

B: Here you go. Is there anything else?

A: _____.

C. PAIRS. Role-play the conversation in Exercise B.

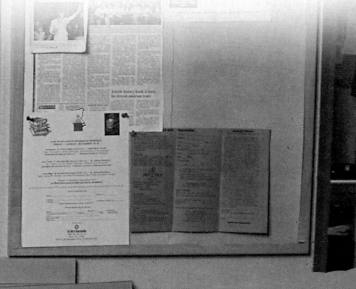

PILATES

**YMCA
IS NOT RESPONSIBLE
FOR VALUABLES**

**PLEASE UTILIZE OUR
LOCKERS**

swim gym **Price List**

GRAMMAR FOCUS

Can for requests

Questions	Affirmative answers	Negative answers
Can I ask you a question?	Sure.	No, sorry.
Can you spell that, please?	Yes, of course.	Sorry, I can't. I'm busy right now.
Can you please help me?	OK.	Sorry, I'm busy.
Can he/she apply for a guest pass?	No problem.	

Discovering grammar

Look at the grammar chart. Complete the grammar rules.

1. Use _____ to make a request.

2. Use _____ to make a request more polite.

Practicing grammar

5 Practice

Write requests and responses. Use *can*, *please*, and a question mark in the requests.
[Note: *X* means *no*; ✔ means *yes*]

1. pick up the eraser on the floor

   A: *Can you pick up the eraser, please?*

   B: *Sure.*

2. give this note to the principal

   A: _____

   B: **X** _____

3. carry my books

   A: _____

   B: **X** _____

4. close the window

   A: _____

   B: ✔ _____

5. turn off the computer

   A: _____

   B: ✔ _____

Learn to learn

Ask for help.

Don't be afraid to ask your teacher or your classmates for help.

A. Look at Exercise 6. Ask yourself: Is there anything that I don't understand? Which part?

B. Ask your teacher or a classmate to help you with that part of the lesson.

For example:

You: Can you help me with Exercise 6, please? *OR* Can you explain Exercise 6 to me, please?

6 Practice

PAIRS. Take turns. Follow the instructions.

1. **A:** (Ask your classmate if you can ask him/her a question.)
   B: (Respond.)
2. **A:** (Ask your classmate to help you with your homework.)
   B: (Respond.)
3. **A:** (Ask your classmate to wait for you.)
   B: (Respond.)
4. **A:** (Ask your classmate to spell his/her name.)
   B: (Respond.)

7 Dialogue

A47 Cover the dialogue and listen. As you listen, write down the events, their dates, and times.

Brian: Andy, look. A volleyball game. Can we go?

Andy: Sure. When is it?

Brian: It's on September 28th. What's this? Peewee baseball . . . Is this baseball for little kids?

Andy: Yup. That's always fun to watch. When is it?

Brian: It's also on the 28th.

Andy: What time?

Brian: In the morning, at 10. The volleyball game starts at 7 P.M.

Andy: Wait a minute. Is today the 21st?

Brian: Yeah. Why?

Andy: Oh no! Yesterday was Caroline's birthday!

Brian: Who's Caroline?

Andy: She's my girlfriend. Oh, man! I'm in big trouble.

8 Comprehension

Answer the questions. Use your notes.

1. What events are on September 28th?
   a volleyball game and peewee baseball

2. What event is in the morning?

3. What event is at seven o'clock at night?

4. What game is at ten o'clock?

5. Whose birthday is on September 20th?

9 Vocabulary

Ordinal numbers

A. **A48** Listen and repeat.

1st first	2nd second	3rd third
4th fourth	5th fifth	6th sixth
7th seventh	8th eighth	9th ninth
10th tenth	11th eleventh	12th twelfth
13th thirteenth	14th fourteenth	15th fifteenth
16th sixteenth	17th seventeenth	18th eighteenth
19th nineteenth	20th twentieth	21st twenty-first

B. **PAIRS.** Take turns. One student says three cardinal numbers at random. The other says the corresponding ordinal numbers.

For example:

A: Three, nine, one   **B:** Third, ninth, first

10 Practice

Have a competition! Go to page 131.

GRAMMAR FOCUS

When/What time/What day + prepositions of time

Questions	Answers
When's the volleyball game?	**On** September 28th.
When's her birthday?	**In** September.
When's her birthday?	**On** Saturday.
What time's the game?	**At** 10:00 in the morning.
What day's the game?	**On** Saturday.

Contractions
When's = When is   What time's = What time is
What day's = What day is

Practicing grammar

11 Practice

PAIRS. Ask and answer the questions.

When's your birthday?

July 23rd.

1. What day is it today?

   _____

2. When's our next English test?

   _____

3. What day is [*name of TV show*] on?

   _____

4. What time is [*name of TV show*] on?

   _____

5. When's your dad's birthday?

   _____

Discovering grammar

Look at the grammar chart. Complete the grammar rules.

1. Use _____ to ask about the date of an event.

2. Use _____ to ask about the exact time of an event.

3. Use _____ to ask about the exact day of an event.

4. Use the preposition _____ with specific dates.

5. Use the preposition _____ with a specific time.

6. Use the preposition _____ with a specific day of the week.

12 Practice

Look at the sentences. Write questions for the underlined parts.

1. Q: *When's Halloween?*
   A: Halloween is <u>on October 31st</u>.

2. Q: _____

   _____

   A: Our drama practice is <u>at 3:30</u> today.

3. Q: _____

   _____

   A: The skateboard competition is <u>on Sunday</u>.

4. Q: _____

   _____

   A: New Year's day is <u>in January</u>.

5. Q: _____

   _____

   A: *Lost* is <u>at 9:00</u> tonight on Channel 5.

13 Practice

A. Write the names of the months in order in the first column of the notebook below.

B. **PAIRS.** Go around the room in pairs. Student 1 talks while Student 2 writes. Student 1 asks as many classmates as possible:

A: When's your birthday?

B: It's on _____.

Student 2 writes the responses in the chart. Which pair collected the most responses?

MONTH	NAME & BIRTHDAY
January	Katherine (January 3) Tomas (January 18)
December	

14 Pronunciation

Intonation patterns in information questions

A. (A49) Listen. Notice how the voice falls on the last content word in information questions.

1. When's the party?

2. When's her birthday?

3. What time's the game?

4. What day's the game?

B. (A50) Listen again and repeat.

15 Communication

Ask about dates and times

A. (A51) Listen to the conversation.

A: When's our <u>history test</u>?

B: It's on <u>November 8th</u>.

A: What day is that?

B: It's Friday.

B. **PAIRS.** Take turns. Ask each other about important dates and times. Use *When's*, *What day is*, and *What time is*.

TEEN TALK

GROUPS. Talk about your favorite TV shows. Ask and answer questions.

Useful language:
- What's your favorite TV show?
- What channel is it on?
- What time and day is it on?
- (Ask your own questions.)

16 Reading

A. Scan the summer dance class schedule. Write the types of dance offered this summer.

salsa , _____, _____, _____, _____, _____, _____, _____

THE SCHOOL OF DANCE
SUMMER SCHEDULE

Monday	Tuesday	Wednesday	Thursday	Friday	Saturday
Salsa for Beginners	Swing Dance for Teens	Ballet	Hip-hop and Funk (Intermediate)	Jazz and Tap Age 14+	NEW! Belly Dance for Teens
Rm. 12	Rm. 30	Rm. 27	Rm. 37	Rm. 25	Rm. 15
Instructor: Elissa	Instructor: Isadora	Instructor: Mario	Instructor: Gino	Instructor: Barry	Instructor: Sofia
First session: June 3rd	First session: June 30th	First session: July 1st	First session: July 15th	First session: August 4th	First session: July 5th
5:00–6:00 P.M.	5:00–7:00 P.M.	5:30–6:30 P.M.	5:30–7:30 P.M.	5:00–6:00 P.M.	5:00–7:00 P.M.

B. PAIRS. Read the summer schedule carefully. Then take turns asking and answering the questions.

1. When's the first session for the salsa class?
   It's on Monday, June 3rd, at 5 P.M.
2. What class is new for this summer?
3. What day and time is ballet class?
4. For what age is tap class?
5. What class is on Tuesdays from 5:00 to 7:00 P.M.?
6. Can beginners enroll in hip-hop class this summer? Why or why not?
7. When are hip-hop and funk classes?

17 Listening

A. (A52) Listen and fill in the form for Annie.

THE SCHOOL OF DANCE

Last name: _Akiyama_   First name: _____

Date of birth: _____   Tel. No: _____

Check your age: _____10–12   _____13–14   _____15–16

Class: _____   Day: _____

B. Exchange work with a classmate. Check the answers.

18 Speaking

PAIRS. Take turns. Ask and answer the following:

- Annie's last name
- her age
- her phone number
- her birthday

For example:

A: What's Annie's last name?
B: It's Akiyama.

19 Writing

A. GROUPS. You own a dance school. Create a poster ad for your dance school. Include the following information:

- the types of dance you're offering
- the instructor for each class
- the days and times for each class
- the phone number to call
- the address of the school

B. GROUPS. Present your poster to the class. Answer any questions your classmates have.

Progress check

Units 3 and 4

> **Test-taking tip:** Budget your time.
> Estimate how much time you will need. Allow a few minutes to review your answers.

Grammar

A. Rewrite the sentences. Use plural nouns. (2 points each)

1. That fax is for you.

   Those faxes are for you.

2. Is this our dictionary?

   _____

3. That man is from Chile.

   _____

4. The box is on the table.

   _____

5. The key is under the desk.

   _____

B. Write sentences using the cues. Use *a* or *an*. (2 points each)

1. Brian / exchange student

   Brian is an exchange student.

2. Eric / student

   _____

3. Liza / teenager

   _____

4. This / easy test

   _____

5. Australia / big country

   _____

C. Complete the sentences with *in*, *on*, or *at*. (1 point each)

1. My birthday is __in__ August.
2. It's _____ August 23rd.
3. Our tap class is _____ Saturday.
4. Let's meet _____ 11:00 in the morning.
5. The game starts _____ 2:00 P.M.
6. The class starts _____ June 5th.

Vocabulary

D. Write the nationality for each country. (1 point each)

1. France _____ _French_ _____
2. Poland _____
3. Japan _____
4. Great Britain _____
5. Costa Rica _____
6. Finland _____

E. Unscramble the letters to find the months. Then write sentences. (3 points each)

1. iparl _____ _April is the fourth month._ _____
2. beeemprst _____
3. uugats _____
4. rebcoot _____
5. hcamr _____

Communication

F. Complete the conversation. (3 points each)

A: _____ _What's your name?_ _____

B: Justin.

A: _____

B: J-U-S-T-I-N.

A: _____

B: 55 Isabel Street, Coral Gables, Florida.

A: _____

B: (305) 555-4177.

A: _____

B: My birthday? It's on March 17th.

> **Now I can . . .**
> ❏ talk about where people are from.
> ❏ ask for personal information.
> ❏ make requests.

5 I have two sisters.

1 Vocabulary

Family members

A. Look at the names in Andy Gibson's family tree. Find each person in the picture. Write the person's name in the tree.

B. (A53) Listen to the family words and repeat.

2 Practice

Guess the family words. Fill in the missing letters to complete them.

1. grandfather and grandmother =
   g <u>r a n d p a r e n t</u> s

2. father and mother = p _ _ _ _ _ s

3. son and daughter = c _ _ _ _ _ _ n

4. grandson and granddaughter =
   g _ _ _ _ _ _ _ _ _ _ _ n

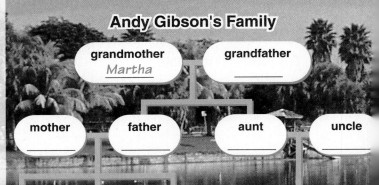

Andy Gibson's Family

| grandmother | grandfather |
| *Martha* | _____ |

mother | father | aunt | uncle

Andy | sister | brother | cousin

Gloria   Charlie   Connie

Robbie   Steve

Bruno

Martha

Liza

Andy

GRAMMAR FOCUS

Possessive forms of nouns

Singular nouns
Andy is Liza**'s** brother.
This is my sister**'s** skateboard.

Plural nouns ending in -s
Liza is the boys**'** sister.
These are my sisters**'** skateboards.

Irregular plural nouns
children**'s** books   women**'s** clothes

Discovering grammar

Look at the grammar chart. Complete the
grammar rules with **'s** or **'**.

1. For most singular nouns (for example,
   sister), add _____.

2. For plural nouns ending in *s* (for example,
   boys), add _____.

3. For irregular plural nouns (for example,
   children), add _____.

Practicing grammar

3 Practice

Add **'s** or **'** to the nouns in parentheses.

1. ___Andy's___ last name is Gibson. (*Andy*)

2. His _____ names are Joe and Gloria.
   (*parents*)

3. The _____ names are Robbie and Andy.
   (*brothers*)

4. Joey is _____ cousin. (*Liza*)

5. Connie is _____ mother. (*Joey*)

6. The _____ names are Martha and Bruno.
   (*grandparents*)

4 Practice

**GROUPS. Take turns. Ask a *Who* question
about three members of Andy's family. The
other members compete to give the correct
answer.**

For example:

Jose: I'll go first. Who's Martha?
Linda: She's Andy's aunt!
Dan: She's Andy's grandmother!
Jose: Dan's right. Who's Steve?

5 Your turn

A. **Draw your family tree on a piece of paper.**

B. **Present your family tree to the class.
Use the possessive form to explain
relationships.**

For example:

These are my grandparents. This is my
grandmother, and this is my grandfather.
They are my father's parents.

6 Dialogue

A54 Cover the dialogue and listen.

Dad: Brian, are you an only child, or do you have any brothers or sisters?

Brian: I don't have any brothers, but I have two sisters.

Liza: How old are they? Do you have any pictures?

Brian: Yeah, I do. Here . . . look. That's Sandy. She's 14. She has blond hair. And this one's Louise. She's 18. Louise has brown hair, like my mom.

Mom: They're very pretty. How about cousins?

Brian: I have eleven cousins.

Robbie: That's a lot! We have only one cousin.

Joey: And that's me!

Robbie: Brian, do you have a girlfriend?

Brian: No, I don't, Robbie.

Robbie: Seriously? Andy has a girlfriend. Her name's Caroline. Liza doesn't have a . . .

Liza: Robbie! Be quiet!

7 Comprehension

A. Cross out the wrong information in each sentence. Correct the sentences.

1. Brian has ~~three~~ _two_ sisters.
2. His sisters' names are Louise and Carla.
3. Louise has black hair.
4. Liza and Joey are sisters.
5. Andy's girlfriend is Sandy.

B. **A55** Check your answers. Read along as you listen again.

8 Useful expressions

A. **A56** Listen and repeat.

- Yeah.
- Seriously?
- And that's me!
- Be quiet!
- That's a lot.

B. Reorder the lines to make a conversation.

____ Seriously?

____ Yeah, I do. I have maybe a hundred DVDs.

_1_ Do you have any DVDs?

____ That's nothing. My uncle has more than 300!

____ A hundred? That's a lot!

C. **PAIRS.** Role-play the conversation.

GRAMMAR FOCUS

The simple present of *have*

Affirmative statements	Negative statements
I/You/We/They **have** two sisters.	I/You/We/They **don't have** any sisters.
He/She **has** a sister.	He/She **doesn't have** any sisters.
It **has** four bedrooms.	It **doesn't have** any bedrooms.

Contractions	
doesn't have = does not have	*don't have = do not have*

Discovering grammar

Look at the grammar chart. Circle the correct answers.

1. Use (*has* / *have*) with *I*, *You*, *We*, and *They*.
2. Use (*has* / *have*) with *He*, *She*, and *It*.
3. Use (*doesn't have* / *don't have*) with *I*, *You*, *We*, and *They*.
4. Use (*doesn't have* / *don't have*) with *He*, *She*, and *It*.
5. Use *any* in (*affirmative* / *negative*) statements.

Practicing grammar

9 Practice

Fill in the blanks with *has*, *have*, *doesn't have*, or *don't have*. Then answer the question.

10 Practice

Write sentences using *has*, *have*, *doesn't have*, or *don't have* and the cues.

1. Brian / two sisters
   _____Brian has two sisters._____

2. He / any brothers
   _____

3. Andy, Liza, and Robbie / a lot of cousins
   _____

4. Joey / any brothers or sisters
   _____

5. Liza / a boyfriend
   _____

6. Sandy and Louise / one brother
   _____

11 Practice

Have a competition! Go to page 131.

WHO AM I?

My name is Rufus. I _____have_____ four brothers and three sisters. We live with different families.

I live with the Garcia family. Mr. and Mrs. Garcia (1) _____ three cats, but they (2) _____ any children. Two of the cats (3) _____ brown eyes. The other cat (4) _____ green eyes.

Our house is big. It has a balcony, but it (5) _____ a backyard. It (6) _____ five bedrooms, but I (7) _____ a bedroom. I (8) _____ a small bed in the living room. Sometimes I sleep on the sofa. The cats (9) _____ any bedrooms either. Sometimes they sleep next to me. We're friends.

I (10) _____ a good life.

Who is Rufus? _____

GRAMMAR FOCUS

The simple present of *have*; *any*

Yes/No questions	Affirmative answers	Negative answers
Do you/they **have any** sisters?	Yes, we/they **do**.	No, we/they **don't**.
Does he/she **have any** sisters?	Yes, he/she **does**.	No, he/she **doesn't**.
Does it **have any** bedrooms?	Yes, it **does**.	No, it **doesn't**.

Questions with *How many*

How many cousins **does** he **have**?	He **has** eleven cousins.
How many cousins **do** they **have**?	They **have** fifteen cousins.

Discovering grammar

Look at the grammar chart. Circle the correct answers.

1. Use *How many* to ask about things you (*can / cannot*) count.
2. Which question is correct? Circle it.
   Does + he + has ten cousins?
   Does + he + have ten cousins?
3. Which question is correct? Circle it.
   How many cousins + does + he + have?
   How many cousins + he + does + has?

Practicing grammar

12 Practice

Complete the questions and answers.

1. Q: ___*Does*___ Rufus _____ brothers and sisters?

   A: Yes, he _____.

2. Q: _____ Mr. and Mrs. Garcia _____ any children?

   A: No, they _____.

3. Q: _____ Rufus _____ a bedroom?

   A: No, he _____.

4. Q: _____ Rufus _____ a good life?

   A: Yes, he _____.

13 Practice

Test your memory about Rufus. Take turns. Ask how many . . .

- brothers and sisters Rufus has
- cats Mr. and Mrs. Garcia have
- cats have brown eyes
- bedrooms the house has

14 Pronunciation

Rising intonation in *Yes/No* questions

A. (A57) **Listen to the questions. Notice how the voice rises on the last syllable of the last word in *Yes/No* questions.**

1. Do you have any cousins?
2. Does he have a girlfriend?
3. Does she have a big family?

B. (A58) **Listen again and repeat the questions in Exercise A.**

15 Communication

Talk about your family

A. (A59) **Listen to the conversation.**

   A: Rose, do you have a big family?
   B: Oh, yeah.
   A: How many brothers and sisters do you have?
   B: I have four brothers and five sisters.
   A: Seriously? That's a big family!
   B: What about cousins? Do you have any?

B. **PAIRS. Take turns asking and answering questions about each other's family.**

16 Vocabulary

Adjectives for physical description

A. Look at the adjectives and the pictures. Write a Harry Potter character next to each adjective.

Harry Potter

Ron Weasley

Hermione Granger

Albus Dumbledore

Draco Malfoy

Cho Chang

Hairstyle		Hair color	
long	_Hermione Granger_	black	_____
medium length	_____	brown	_____
short	_____	light brown	_____
straight	_____	red	_____
wavy	_____	blond	_____
curly	_____	white	_____

B. PAIRS. Ask *Yes/No* questions about three of the characters.

For example:

A: Does Draco have curly, blond hair?

B: No, he doesn't. He has straight, blond hair.

Learn to learn

Group new vocabulary into categories.

Putting words into categories can help you learn words faster.

A. GROUPS. One way of learning words by categories is to make a word web. Complete the word webs with words from this unit.

straight

hairstyles

sister

family words for women

B. Make word webs for these: *family words for men* and *family words for both men and women*. Then complete your word webs.

17 Listening

A60 **Listen to each description. Guess who the person is. Choose your answers from the characters in the box.**

Dobby	Hagrid	Minerva McGonagall	Ron Weasley

Description 1 _____

Description 2 _____

Description 3 _____

Description 4 _____

GROUPS. Talk about the Harry Potter characters.

Useful language:
- Who's your favorite Harry Potter character?
- My favorite is _____.
- Can you describe him/her?
- He/She has _____ hair (eyes).

18 Writing

A. Think of a favorite person. This person can be a family member, a friend, a teacher, a book or movie character, or an entertainer. Write a description of this person.

B. PAIRS. Read your classmate's paragraph. Circle any errors. Use the Peer editing checklist on page 134 to help you with your comments.

Putting it together *At Caroline's*

A. (A61) **Cover the dialogue. Listen to the conversation. What are the ways Andy can communicate with Caroline?** _____, _____, _____

1.

Oh, it's you.

I'm really sorry I missed your birthday. I'm very busy. Brian's here.

2.

I know, but you have a cell phone. And, oh yeah, your phone has text messaging, too. And you also have e-mail.

Come on, Caroline.

3.

So, this Brian. Is he cute?

I don't know. But he has blue eyes and blond hair. He's from Australia.

4.

Ooh. An Australian with blue eyes! I like that.

I have brown eyes. Do you like brown eyes?

5.

Well, yeah. So, when can I meet Brian?

6.

He's busy. Hey, I'm still your boyfriend, remember?

And you don't have time for your girlfriend, remember?

B. (A62) **Check your answers. Read along as you listen again. Then discuss the questions.**

- Is Caroline a good girlfriend? Why or why not?
- Is Andy a good boyfriend? Why or why not?

Game 2 *Spelling bee*

Steps:

1. Work in teams. Your teacher will write the team numbers on the board.

2. Team 1 Player A stands. The teacher reads a word. If asked, the teacher can repeat the word once more. The player has 5 seconds to begin spelling the word.

3. If Team 1 Player A can spell the word correctly, he or she can write the word under his or her team number on the board. The teacher then reads a new word to Team 2 Player A. If Team 1 Player A cannot spell the word correctly, the teacher reads the word to the other teams, in order, until it is spelled correctly.

4. The game continues until all the words have been written on the board. The team with the most words wins!

Useful language

- Congratulations!
- Great job!
- Oh well, that was a hard one.

bedroom	house	tired	computer	backyard	school
phone	practice	exchange	classmate	backpack	favorite
uncle	wavy	straight	grandson	fifteenth	Chinese
volleyball	boxes	cousin	countries	wallet	skateboard
awesome	Australian	favorite	dictionary	bicycle	information
characters	twelfth	addresses	February	principal	daughter

Project 2   *A snapshot of someone I like*

Write a magazine article about a person you like. The person can be someone famous—an actor, a singer, or an athlete. Or it can be a family member or a friend. Choose photos to go with your article. Then share your article with your classmates. Use the article and steps below as a guide.

Shakira

1. Write about a person you like. Say why you like him or her.

I really like Shakira. She's a great singer and songwriter. She has a lot of hit songs. My favorite songs are "La Tortura" and "Don't Bother." I like her videos, too.

2. Write about where the person is from and where he or she lives now. Tell about his or her family and friends.

Shakira is from Colombia. Her parents live in Barranquilla, but now Shakira lives in Miami. She has a boyfriend. His name is Antonio de la Rúa. He's from Argentina.

3. Describe the person.

Shakira is very pretty. She has long blonde wavy hair and brown eyes. She likes fashion, and she has a lot of cool clothes.

4. Write about other things you know about that person.

Shakira speaks Spanish and English. She has many music awards. She's very popular all over the world. And she's a fabulous dancer.

6 I'm not crazy about hip-hop.

1 Dialogue

A63 **Cover the dialogue and listen.**

Brian: So, how are things with Caroline?

Andy: Not good.

Brian: When can I meet her?

Andy: I have no idea. Soon, I guess. Let's not talk about her, OK? Do you have an iPod, Brian?

Brian: Nope. I can't afford one.

Andy: Me neither. So, what kind of music do you like?

Brian: It depends. I listen to all kinds of music, but I'm not crazy about hip-hop music.

Andy: Why not? I love hip-hop, especially rap.

Brian: I don't know. I'm just not into it. What about Liza and Robbie? Do they like rap, too?

Andy: Liza doesn't like rap. She can't stand it. She prefers pop music, and Robbie likes anything loud and noisy. He hates slow music.

Brian: I don't blame him.

2 Comprehension

A. **Write the kind of music each person likes and doesn't like.**

	Likes	Doesn't like
Brian	All kinds	
Andy		
Liza		
Robbie		

B. **A64** **Check your answers. Read along as you listen again.**

Learning goals

Communication
Talk about likes and dislikes

Grammar
The simple present of *like*
Object pronouns

Vocabulary
Ways of expressing likes and dislikes

3 Useful expressions

A. (A65) **Listen and repeat.**

- How are things?
- Not good.
- I have no idea.
- I guess.
- Nope.
- Me neither.
- I'm not crazy about it.
- Why not?
- I don't know.
- I'm just not into it.

B. Complete the conversations with expressions from the box.

1. **A:** How are things with you?

   B: _____

2. **A:** Do you like hip-hop music?

   B: _____

3. **A:** I can't afford to buy an iPod.

   B: _____

4 Vocabulary

Ways of expressing likes and dislikes

A. (A66) **Listen and repeat.**

Expressing likes ☺
- I love rap music.
- I like music.

- We're into music.

- He's crazy about rock music.

Expressing dislikes ☹
- I hate rap music.
- I don't like classical music.

- We're not into hip-hop music.

- She can't stand rap music.

B. Complete the sentences with kinds of music or groups/singers you like and don't like.

1. I'm into _____.

2. I'm crazy about _____.

3. I hate _____.

4. I can't stand _____.

5 Pronunciation

The sound /z/

A. (A67) **Listen and repeat.**

- does
- doesn't
- jazz
- bands

B. (A68) **Listen to the conversation.**

A: Does Liza listen to jazz?
B: No, she doesn't.
A: Does she like boy bands?
B: Yes, she does. She's crazy about them.

C. (A69) **PAIRS. Listen again. Then role-play the conversation.**

GRAMMAR FOCUS

The simple present of *like*

Affirmative statements	Negative statements	Yes/No questions	Short answers
I You } **like** music.	I You } **don't like** music.	Does he **like** rap music?	Yes, he **does**./ No, he **doesn't**.
He She } **likes** music.	He She } **doesn't like** rap music.	Do they **like** rap music?	Yes, they **do**./ No, they **don't**.
We You They } **like** music.	We You They } **don't like** rap music.	**Information questions**	**Answers**
		What kind of music **does** she **like**?	She **likes** pop music.
		What kind of music **do** you **like**?	I **like** rock music.

Discovering grammar

Look at the grammar chart. Circle the correct answers.

1. In affirmative statements . . .
   a. use (*like* / *likes*) with *He* or *She*.
   b. use (*like* / *likes*) with *I, You, We,* or *They*.
2. In negative statements . . .
   a. use (*doesn't* / *don't*) with *He* or *She*.
   b. use (*doesn't* / *don't*) with *I, You, We,* or *They*.
3. In *Yes/No* questions . . .
   a. use (*do* / *does*) with *He, She,* or *It*.
   b. use (*do* / *does*) with *I, You, We,* or *They*.

Practicing grammar

6 Practice

Complete the sentences with the correct forms of the verbs in parentheses.

1. Brian and Andy (*like*) ___like___ music.
2. Andy (*like*) _____ rap.
3. Brian (*not like*) _____ rap music.
4. Liza (*hate*) _____ rap music.
5. She (*prefer*) _____ pop music.
6. Robbie (*like*) _____ loud music.
7. Many teenagers (*like*) _____ rap.
8. Most teenagers (*not like*) _____ sentimental songs.

7 Practice

Read the answers. Write *Yes/No* questions with *like*.

1. ___Do you like English?___

   Yes, I do. I like English.

2. _____

   No, she doesn't. My mother doesn't like ballet.

3. _____

   Yes, they do. Our teachers love classical music.

4. _____

   Yes, they do. My friends love sports.

5. _____

   No, he doesn't. My father hates scary movies.

6. _____

   No, we don't. We don't like loud music.

8 Practice

A. Make a list of six popular singers or groups. Write them in the chart below.

B. Take a survey. Ask five classmates about the performers on your list.

For example:

A: Do you like Christina Aguilera?
B: Yes, I do./No, I don't.

Write your classmates' first names in the appropriate columns.

Likes	Doesn't Like	Singer/Group
Tracy	Austin	Christina Aguilera

GROUPS. Talk about music, bands, and singers you like or don't like. Use *like, love, prefer, don't like, can't stand*, or *hate* in your conversation.

Useful language:
• I like . . .
• I prefer . . .
• I love . . .
• I can't stand . . .
• I hate . . .
• I don't like . . .

9 Your turn

GROUPS. Talk about the singers in the chart. Ask each other these questions.

• Do you like any of them?
• Who do you like?
• Do you know any of his or her songs?
• Can you sing a few lines from the song?

10 Communication

Talk about likes and dislikes

A. (A70) **Listen to the conversation.**

A: I love <u>Mariah Carey's new album</u>.
B: Really? I hate it.
A: You do? What kind of music do you like?
B: Well, I'm into <u>rap</u>. I like <u>Kanye West</u>.
A: Yuck. I can't stand <u>rap</u>.

B. **PAIRS. Role-play the conversation. Replace the names with your favorites.**

11 Dialogue

(A71) **Cover the dialogue and listen.**

Caroline: Hello?

Andy: Hello? Is this Caroline?

Caroline: Hi, Andy.

Andy: Are you still mad at me?

Caroline: Maybe. What do you want?

Andy: Do you still want to meet Brian?

Caroline: It depends. Does he want to meet me?

Andy: Of course he does.

Caroline: When can I meet him?

Andy: How about tomorrow? Would you like to come with us to the movies?

Caroline: *Us?* What do you mean by "us"?

Andy: Brian, Liza, Robbie, and me.

Caroline: You mean, the entire family? No, thanks.

12 Comprehension

A. Answer the questions.

1. Is Caroline nice to Andy?
2. Does Brian want to meet Caroline?
3. Does Caroline want to meet Brian?

B. **(A72)** **Check your answers. Read along as you listen again.**

GRAMMAR FOCUS

Object pronouns

Subject pronouns	Object pronouns	Examples
I	me	me.
You	you	you.
He	him	him.
She	her	her.
It	it	Liza likes it.
We	us	us.
You	you	you.
They	them	them.

Object pronouns after prepositions

Are you still mad **at me**?

Would you like to come **with us**?

Discovering grammar

Look at the grammar chart. Circle the correct answers.

1. Object pronouns go (*before* / *after*) a verb.
2. *It* and *You* (*have* / *don't have*) the same subject and object forms.

Practicing grammar

13 Practice

Complete the sentences with object pronouns.

1. Shakira is great. I love _____*her*_____.
2. This new ice cream flavor is really good. I like _____.
3. Paris Hilton is annoying. I can't stand _____.
4. Operas are boring. I don't like _____.
5. You're cute. I like _____. Do you like _____, too?
6. There's Brad Pitt! Can you see _____?

14 Practice

Play a game! Go to page 131.

15 Reading

A. Read the article quickly. Underline the sentence that expresses the main idea.
- a. Teenagers are into hip-hop.
- b. Parents can't stand teen music.
- c. Adults worry that music influences their children's behavior.

B. A73 Read the article as you listen.

Is today's music bad for kids?

Today's parents are worried. Their children and their iPods are inseparable. Wherever they go, teenagers listen to music on their iPods. The problem is not the iPods but the kinds of music teenagers listen to. Most teenagers are into rap and other kinds of hip-hop music. Why is this a problem? Listen to the lyrics of many rap songs. They're often about drugs, sex, and violence.

But does music influence young people's behavior? For example, do teenagers who listen to rap songs about violence become violent? Do those who listen to rock, heavy metal, and rap become drug users?

There are many different opinions. Some say singers and their songs affect the behavior of young people. They say that music with violent lyrics is the reason some young people commit crimes, and some teenagers do drugs because their favorite singers do the same thing. The singers say it is ridiculous to blame them and their songs for what teenagers choose to do. They say it is the responsibility of parents to raise their kids well. Singers are not babysitters. In one of his raps, Eminem asks, "Where were the parents at?" In other words, Eminem is blaming the parents, not the singers or their songs, when kids go wrong.

The debate continues. What about you? Do you think today's music is bad for you?

16 Comprehension

Write *True* or *False*. Circle the wrong information in the false statements.

According to the article . . .

_____ 1. Teenagers listen to music all the time.

_____ 2. Parents are worried because iPods are expensive.

_____ 3. Most teenagers like hip-hop music.

_____ 4. Many rap songs talk about drugs, sex, and violence.

_____ 5. Singers agree that they influence the behavior of young people.

Learn to learn

Read without understanding every word.

When you read a text, don't worry if you don't understand the meaning of every word. First, read the whole text to get the main ideas. Then try to work out the meanings of unfamiliar words.

PAIRS. Underline the words you don't understand in the article. Then try to guess the meanings of some of these words. Use a dictionary to check if you were right.

17 Listening

A. (A74) **Listen to the interview. What kinds of music do the teenagers like? Put a check (✔) before the ones you hear.**

_____ Rock	_____ Jazz
_____ Techno	_____ Pop
_____ R&B	_____ Country
✔ Hip-hop/Rap	_____ Punk rock

B. (A75) **Listen again. Complete the sentences with words from the box.**

Ashley	Eminem	~~music~~
CDs	Mario	punk

1. The three teenagers listen to __*music*__ all the time.

2. _____ listens to music when doing homework.

3. Mario likes rap, rock, and _____ music.

4. _____ likes Avril Lavigne and Kelly Clarkson.

5. Karen's parents don't like songs by _____.

6. The kids never listen to their parents' _____.

18 Speaking

GROUPS. **Talk about your favorite types of music.**

1. Do you listen to music a lot?
2. Where and when do you listen to music?
3. What kinds of music do you listen to?
4. What is more important to you: the lyrics or the melody?
5. Do you try to understand the lyrics of your favorite songs?

Progress check   *Units 5 and 6*

Test-taking tip: Ask for help and clarification.
Raise your hand and ask for help if you don't understand the test directions.

Grammar

A. Complete the sentences with the correct forms of the verbs in parentheses. Use contractions when possible. (1 point each)

1. I (*not have*) ___don't have___ any sisters.

2. Brian (*have*) _____ two sisters.

3. He (*not have*) _____ any brothers.

4. My mom (*have*) _____ a lot of cousins.

5. I (*not have*) _____ an uncle.

6. You (*not have*) _____ a test today.

B. Write *Yes/No* questions for the answers. (2 points each)

1. **A:** ___Do you like video games?___

   B: Yes, I do. I like video games.

2. **A:** _____

   B: No, we don't. We don't like classical music.

3. **A:** _____

   B: Yes, she does. She loves sushi.

4. **A:** _____

   B: No, they don't. They don't like sports.

5. **A:** _____

   B: No, he doesn't. He doesn't like rap. He prefers rock.

6. **A:** _____

   B: Yes, they do. They're crazy about jazz.

C. Write the possessive forms of the nouns in parentheses. (1 point each)

1. What's your (*sister*) ___sister's___ name?

2. Is this your (*brother*) _____ room?

3. All my (*friends*) _____ parents are so cool.

4. (*Brian*) _____ family is in Australia.

5. Their (*grandparents*) _____ house is beautiful.

Vocabulary

D. Match the phrases with the words. (1 point each)

1. my mother's father
2. my father's sister
3. my uncle's children
4. my parents' daughter
5. my mother and father
6. my mother's brother
7. my father's mother and father
8. my parents' son

   a. my aunt
   b. my sister
   c. my grandparents
   d. my grandfather
   e. my uncle
   f. my parents
   g. my brother
   h. my cousin

E. Answer the questions. (3 points each)

1. Do you like vegetables?

   ☺ / love ___Yes, I do. I love them.___

2. Is your brother into jazz?

   ☺ / love _____

3. Does your friend like sports?

   ☺ / love _____

4. Is your dad into heavy metal?

   ☹ / can't stand _____

5. Do you like movies?

   ☹ / hate _____

Communication

F. PAIRS. Take turns. Answer the questions about your family. (3 points each)

- Do you have any brothers or sisters? (Note: If your answer is "no," talk about your cousins or your parents.)
- Do they like music?
- What kinds of music do they like?
- Who are their favorite singers?

Now I can . . .
❏ talk about my family.
❏ describe people.
❏ talk about likes and dislikes.

Potter Teens

Daniel Radcliffe plays Harry Potter. Dan lives in London, England, and has two dogs, Binka and Nugget. Dan loves music. In fact, he plays the bass guitar. He's into classic punk and rock. Some of his favorite musicians are David Bowie, the Rolling Stones, and the Red Hot Chili Peppers. In his leisure time, Dan writes stories and goes to the movies. His favorite movies include *Moulin Rouge* and *Crash*. For exercise, Dan runs and works out. His favorite sport is soccer. There's a rumor that Emma Watson is Dan's girlfriend, but he says they're just friends.

Emma Watson plays Hermione Granger. When she's not at boarding school or making movies, Emma lives with her mother and younger brother. They call her "Em" for short. Em and her brother have two cats, Bubbles and Domino. In her leisure time, she plays hockey, tennis, and rounders—a British game similar to baseball. Em also spends a lot of time listening to music, especially pop. Her favorite singers include Alanis Morissette, Shakira, and Suzanne Vega. She also likes watching movies, and her favorite actor is Brad Pitt. She thinks he's gorgeous.

Rupert Grint (Ron Weasley)

Lives: Hertfordshire, England, with
  his (1) _____, one
  younger (2) _____, three
  younger (3) _____

Leisure time: swims, plays golf,
  rides his (4) _____, paints

Favorite sport: (5) _____

Also likes: music and
  (6) _____

Music: likes all kinds of music, but
  his favorite is (7) _____;
  plays the guitar

Movies: (8) _____ Jim Carrey
  movies; a favorite is **Dumb and
  Dumber**

Hates: spiders (just like
  (9) _____)

1 Reading

> **Reading skill:** Personalizing
> Think about how you are similar to the people or characters in an article. You will enjoy the reading more and remember it better.

A. Read the article. What do you have in common with Daniel and Emma? Write a ✔ above three things that are similar and an X above three things that are different, like this:

  ✔   X
Dan loves music. In fact, he plays the bass guitar.
(=I love music. I don't play the bass guitar.)

B. How much can you remember from the reading? Write a _D_ next to the things that are about Daniel. Write _E_ next to those that are true about Emma.

1. __E__ has two cats
2. _____ plays the bass guitar
3. _____ lives with mother and younger brother
4. _____ plays hockey, tennis, and rounders
5. _____ runs and works out
6. _____ into classic punk and rock
7. _____ likes soccer
8. _____ likes Shakira and Brad Pitt

C. Read the article again and check your answers.

2 Listening

Ⓐ76 Listen to an interview with Tessa James, a big fan of Rupert Grint. Complete the information on the left about Rupert.

3 Speaking

PAIRS. Discuss the following questions.

1. How are you similar to Daniel, Emma, and Rupert?
2. How are you different?

4 Writing

Write a paragraph about Rupert Grint based on the information on the left. Use the paragraphs on Daniel Radcliffe and Emma Watson as a guide.

7 Can you count?

Learning goals

Communication
Talk about abilities
Ask for permission

Grammar
Imperatives
Can to talk about abilities

Vocabulary
Clock times

1 Dialogue

B1 **Cover the dialogue and listen.**

Andy: Look who's here! Hi, Joey.
Joey: Is this a bad time to come?
Andy: No, no. It's OK. What time is it?
Joey: One o'clock. Are you guys going out?
Liza: Well, yeah.
Andy: Be quiet, Liza! Don't be rude.
Brian: Joey! It's good to see you!
Joey: Thanks.
Brian: Hey, why's your name *Joey*?
Joey: It's short for Josephine.
Brian: Oh, cool. Andy, what time does the movie start?
Joey: What movie? Can I come, too?
Liza: Joey, we can't all fit in the car!
Andy: Don't listen to her, Joey.
Liza: Oh, all right. Hurry up.

2 Comprehension

A. Circle the correct answers.

1. Liza is (*happy* / *not happy*) to see Joey.
2. Brian (*likes* / *hates*) the name *Joey*.
3. Joey (*wants* / *doesn't want*) to go to the movies.
4. Andy (*is nice* / *isn't nice*) to Joey.
5. Liza (*is nice* / *isn't nice*) to Joey.

B. B2 **Read along as you listen again. Check your answers.**

3 Useful expressions

A. (B3) **Listen and repeat.**

- Look who's here!
- Hurry up.
- It's good to see you.
- All right.
- Is this a bad time to come?
- No. It's OK.

B. Complete the dialogues with expressions from Exercise A.

A: _Look who's here_! Hi, [*Joey*].

B: Hi, [*Brian*]. Are you busy? _____

A: No, no. It's OK. _____

B: Nice to see you, too. Are you going out?

A: Yeah, to the mall. Would you like to come?

B: All right.

A: Come on. _____

C. PAIRS. Role-play the conversation in Exercise B. Replace the names with your classmates' names.

4 Vocabulary

Clock times

A. (B4) **Look at the clock as you listen and repeat.**

ten o'clock
five after ten
ten after ten
a quarter after ten
twenty after ten
twenty-five after ten

ten-thirty/half past ten
twenty-five to eleven
twenty to eleven
a quarter to eleven
ten to eleven
five to eleven

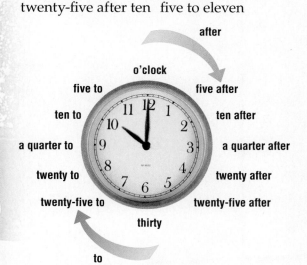

B. PAIRS. Look at the clocks. Take turns asking each other for the time.

For example:

A: What time is it?

B: It's a quarter after eleven.

GRAMMAR FOCUS

Imperatives

Affirmative	Negative
Look who's here!	**Don't look!**

Uses of the imperative

Look out! (*for exclamations and warnings*)
Be quiet! (*for orders*)
Please **help** me. (*for polite requests*)
Pull the door, then **lock** it. (*for instructions*)

Discovering grammar

Look at the grammar chart. Circle the correct answers.

1. An affirmative imperative starts with a (*verb / noun*).
2. (*Do / Don't*) comes first in a negative imperative.
3. Use the (*past tense / base form*) of a verb in an imperative.

Practicing grammar

5 Practice

A. **Write five affirmative classroom commands. Use a period or an exclamation point (!).**

1. <u>*Open* your books!</u>
2. _____
3. _____
4. _____
5. _____
6. _____

B. **Underline the verbs in Exercise A.**

C. **Rewrite the commands in Exercise A as negative commands.**

1. <u>*Don't open your books!*</u>
2. _____
3. _____
4. _____
5. _____
6. _____

D. **PAIRS. Student A, give a command from Exercise A. Student B, act out the command. Take turns giving and acting out commands.**

6 Practice

GROUPS. Have a competition! Go to page 132.

TEEN TALK

A. **GROUPS. Talk about school. Discuss these questions: Is your school a friendly place? Do you like being at school? Explain your answer.**

Useful language:
- Umm, not really./Maybe.
- Well, it's OK.
- I like/don't like school.
- Because of the homework.
- Because I see my friends at school.
- Because some students aren't nice.
- Yeah.

B. **GROUPS. Make a list of ten Dos and Don'ts for students and teachers to make your school a better and more enjoyable place. Share your list with the class.**

1. Be nice to everybody.
2. Don't be rude.
3.
4.
5.
6.
7.
8.
9.
10.

7 Dialogue

(B5) **Cover the dialogue and listen.**

Joey: I'll buy our tickets.

Robbie: Can I go with you, Joey? Please?

Joey: Sure. But first, let's count the money. You can count money, right?

Robbie: Yeah, I can.

Joey: OK. Count this for me.

Robbie: OK. One . . . two . . . twenty . . . thirty . . . forty. Fifty dollars.

Joey: Good. Now, which movie do we want?

Robbie: *Spider-Man, The Final Chapter*!

Joey: Right. So look up there at the movie schedules. Can you find our movie on the list?

Robbie: Yeah. It's at . . . 2:30.

Joey: Good job, Robbie. Now tell the lady what you want.

Robbie: Hello. Five tickets for *Spider-Man* at 2:30, please.

Woman: Here you go. Enjoy the movie.

Robbie: Thanks.

8 Comprehension

A. Write the answers.

1. How much money do they have for the tickets? ___Fifty dollars.___

2. What movie does the group want to see? _____

3. What time does the movie start? _____

4. How many tickets does Robbie buy? _____

B. (B6) **Read along as you listen again. Check your answers.**

GRAMMAR FOCUS

Can to talk about abilities

Affirmative statements
I **can speak** English.

Negative statements
They **can't speak** English.

Yes/No questions
Can you **speak** English?
Can he **speak** German?

Short answers
Yes, I **can**./No, I **can't**.
Yes, he **can**./No, he **can't**.

Information questions
What languages **can** you **speak**?

Who **can speak** English?

Answers
We **can speak** Portuguese
and English.
I **can speak** English.

Contraction
can't ➜ cannot

Discovering grammar

Look at the grammar chart.
Complete the rules.

1. Use _____ + the base
   form of a verb to talk about
   abilities.

2. The full form of *can't* is

   _____ .

Practicing grammar

9 Practice

PAIRS. Look at the picture. Take turns. Ask who can do each activity below.

- speak English
- drive
- act
- ride a bike
- draw
- play soccer
- swim
- dance
- Rollerblade
- sing
- play the guitar
- skateboard

For example:

   A: Who can speak English?
   B: Jim can speak English. Who can sing?

10 Practice

A. **GROUPS.** Play a memory game with four classmates.

For example:

A: I can play the drums.

B: Maria can play the drums. I can ride a bike.

C: Maria can play the drums. Trish can ride a bike. I can dance the samba.

B. Have a representative tell the class what each of your group members can do.

11 Pronunciation

The /æ/ sound in *can* and *can't*

A. (B7) **Listen and repeat.**

can   can't   act
rap   dance   add

A: Can you rap?   **B:** Yes, I can.
A: Can you dance?   **B:** No, I can't.
A: Can you act?   **B:** Yes, I can.
A: Can you add ½ and ¼? **B:** No, I can't.

B. (B8) **Listen again. Then practice the conversations.**

12 Your turn

A. Find someone who can do these activities by asking, "Can you . . . ?" Write the student's name next to the ability.

1. play the piano _____

2. break-dance _____

3. whistle a tune _____

4. skate _____

5. cook _____

6. sing a song in a foreign language

   _____

7. rap _____

8. do the moonwalk _____

9. swim _____

10. do a belly dance _____

B. Share your findings with the class.

Learn to learn

Have a *can-do* attitude.
Think positively. Say "I can," not "I can't."

A. Think about your English skills. What can you do in English? Check (✔) the boxes.

❏ I can speak some English.

❏ I can understand audiotapes in English.

❏ I can pronounce English words well.

❏ I can understand simple readings in English.

❏ I can speak in front of the class.

❏ I can write simple sentences in English.

B. **PAIRS.** Compare your results. Choose one skill you didn't check. What can you do to help each other improve that skill?

For example:
We can practice speaking English together.

13 Communication

Ask for permission

• You can also use *can* to ask for permission.

A. (B9) **Listen to the conversation.**

> **Robbie:** Can I come in, Liza?
> **Liza:** Sure.
> **Robbie:** *[After 5 minutes]* Can I play a game on your computer?
> **Liza:** Not right now, Robbie. I'm busy.

B. **PAIRS.** Student A, ask if you can borrow or use one of your classmate's things. Student B, say *No* because you're using it. Switch roles. This time, Student A, say *Yes*.

14 Practice

A. **PAIRS.** Compete with another pair. Make a list of questions asking for permission that are commonly used in class.

For example:

Can I erase the board?

_____

_____

_____

_____

B. Compare your list with that of another pair. Who wrote the most questions?

68   Unit 7

Putting it together   *At the amusement park*

A. Before you listen, read the dialogue. Fill in the missing responses.

1

That was a fun movie! Hey, Brian, can you drive?

Would you like me to ask Dad?

(1) _____. Sorry. Why?

It'd be fun to go to the amusement park tomorrow.

2

Really? Great! Uh, can I come in for a few minutes?

(2) _____, Joey. It's late, and we're tired.

Oh, OK. Andy, call me tomorrow, OK?

(3) _____.

3 Sunday afternoon

I can't wait to go inside!

Me, too.

Guys, wait! Let's wait for Dad and Robbie.

OK. Wait here. I'll go get the tickets.

4

It's already one o'clock. Better hurry.

I'll be right back.

Well, can we go to the zoo instead?

That was quick.

There's a problem, guys. The park's closed.

6

Good idea. Let's tell Dad.

I'm really sorry.

B. (B10) **Listen to the conversation. Check your answers.**

Unit 7   **69**

8 I always get up at six-thirty.

1 Reading

B11 Read along as you listen to Brian's description of his typical day.

Learning goals

Communication
Talk about daily routines

Grammar
Sequence words: *first, then, after that, next, finally*
Adverbs of frequency
How often?

Vocabulary
Daily routines

Brian's Typical Day

Every morning, on a school day, my alarm goes off at 6:30. But I usually turn it off and close my eyes again. Of course, it's never easy to go back to sleep after the alarm goes off, so I get up.

I do the same things every day. First, I take a shower and get dressed for school. Then I eat breakfast. After that, I brush my teeth. I sometimes have cereal. But I usually just grab a banana and eat it at the bus stop. My bus leaves at exactly 7:30.

School starts at 8:00. I'm never late for school. Lunch break is at 12:00. On nice days, my friends and I sometimes sit outside. Classes end at 3:00, but I never get home until after 6:00. I am on the track and field team, and I practice after school. After practice, I usually go to the gym.

On Saturdays, my school team often competes with teams from other schools. My dad always watches me when I compete. I'm always tired after a competition, but I don't mind it. I love running.

Sunday is my favorite day. It's usually my lazy day, and I love it.

2 Comprehension

A. Match the sentences with the pictures.

_5_ **1.** Brian's alarm goes off at 6:30.

____ **2.** He takes the bus to school.

____ **3.** School starts at 8:00.

____ **4.** He has lunch at school.

____ **5.** On Saturdays, he competes with students from other schools.

B. Answer the questions.

1. What time does Brian get up?

2. What does Brian have for breakfast?

3. What does he do after school?

4. What sport does Brian like?

3 Pronunciation

The pronunciation of –s and –es

A. (B12) **Listen and repeat.**

/s/	/z/	/ɪz/
eats	goes	watches
wakes	leaves	brushes

B. (B13) **Listen. Circle the verbs with the /z/ or /ɪz/ sound.**

1. Brian wakes up at 6:30. He leaves home at 7:30.

2. He goes to high school. He takes the bus to school.

3. He gets home at 6:30. He watches TV.

C. (B14) **Listen again and repeat.**

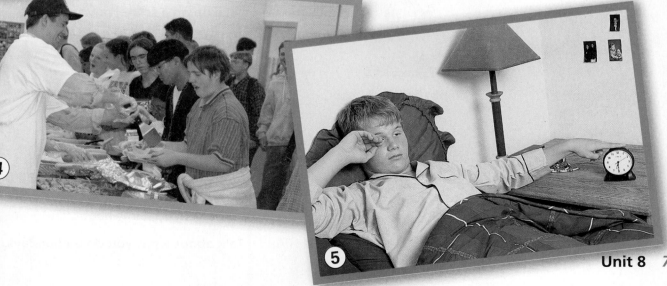

4 Vocabulary

Daily routines

A. Number the activities 1 to 12 according to your routine on school days.

B. PAIRS. Compare your routines.

____ take a shower

____ go to school

_1_ get up

____ eat or have breakfast

____ eat or have dinner

____ do homework

____ brush my teeth

____ get home from school

____ watch TV

____ comb/brush my hair

____ go to bed

____ get dressed

GRAMMAR FOCUS

Sequence words

First, the alarm rings. **Then** I turn it off. **After that**, I get up.

First, she takes a shower. **Next**, she gets dressed. **Then** she has breakfast. **After that**, she brushes her teeth. **Finally**, she leaves the house.

Discovering grammar

Look at the grammar chart. Answer the questions.

1. What are some common sequence words?

_____, _____, _____,

_____, _____

2. What punctuation can you use after some sequence words? _____

Practicing grammar

5 Practice

Write three more things Brian does after he wakes up on a school day.

1. _*First, Brian takes a shower.*_____
2. _____
3. _____
4. _____

6 Your turn

PAIRS. Tell your classmate three things you do after you wake up on a school day.

For example: First, I take a shower.

7 Communication

Talk about your routines

A. (B15) Listen and read.

A: What do you do on Sundays?
B: Nothing much. First, I check my e-mail. Then I text my friends. After that, I call up my best friend. How about you?

B. PAIRS. Talk about what you do on Sundays.

GRAMMAR FOCUS

Adverbs of frequency; *How often?*

0%   100%

always
usually
often
sometimes
rarely/seldom
never

How often do you arrive late to school?

I'm **always** late for school.
I'm **usually** late for school.
I'm **often** late for school.

I'm **sometimes** late for school.
I'm **rarely/seldom** late for school.
I'm **never** late for school.

Positions of frequency adverbs

With *be*
I'm **sometimes** late for school.
Dana **is never** late for school.

With other verbs
I **sometimes wake up** late.
Carlos **never wakes up** late.

Discovering grammar

Look at the grammar chart. Circle the correct answers.

1. Adverbs of frequency tell (*how well* / *how often*) an activity is done.
2. *Never* and *often* are examples of (*adverbs* / *adjectives*).
3. Adverbs of frequency come (*before* / *after*) a form of the verb *be*.
4. They come (*before* / *after*) all other verbs.

Practicing grammar

8 Practice

Insert the adverbs of frequency in the sentences. Then rewrite the sentences.

1. My teacher is ^always^ early. (*always*) _____ My teacher is always early. _____

2. I check my e-mail. (*often*) _____

3. Brian is late. (*never*) _____

4. We study together. (*sometimes*) _____

5. They have lunch together. (*usually*) _____

6. My friends are at my house. (*always*) _____

7. I am late for school. (*sometimes*) _____

9 Practice

A. Find one student who does each of the activities below. Write his or her name on the line.

For example:

Q: How often do you sing in the shower? *OR* How often do you arrive late to school?

1. usually sings in the shower.

   _____

2. never arrives late to school

   _____

3. always does homework

   _____

4. often gets hungry during class

   _____

5. usually falls alseep in class

   _____

6. rarely plays sports

   _____

B. Share your findings with the class.

10 Practice

Play a game! Go to page 132.

GROUPS. Talk about how often you do things. Choose from the activities below or use your own ideas.

- dance
- sing in the shower
- call your grandparents
- go to bed early
- help in the kitchen
- walk to school

- go to parties
- speak English outside class
- go to the library
- go shopping on weekends
- go to the movies

Useful language:
- How often do you . . . ?
- Really?
- That's interesting!

- Why not?
- Because . . .
- No way! / Seriously?

11 Practice

PAIRS. Complete the questionnaire for your classmate by asking questions. Put a check (✔) in the appropriate column.

For example:

A: What do you have for breakfast?

B: I always have cereal and milk. I sometimes have bread and butter.

A: Do you have coffee for breakfast?

B: No. I never have coffee.

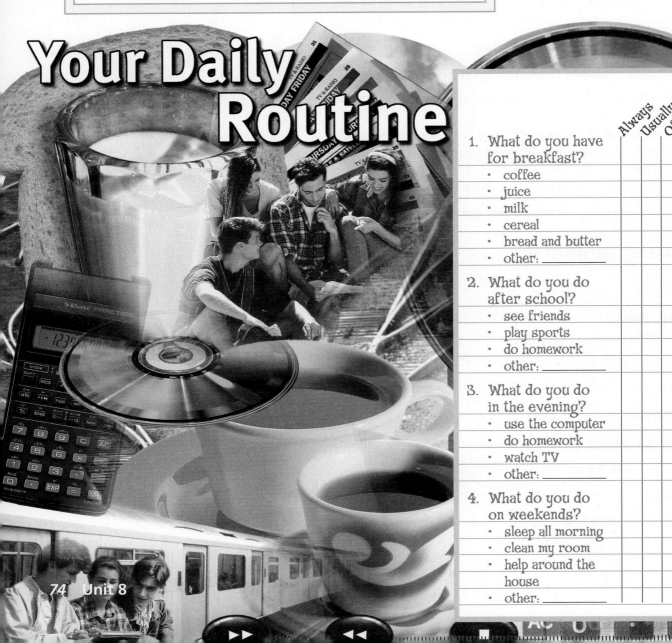

Your Daily Routine

	Always	Usually	Often	Sometimes	Rarely	Never
1. What do you have for breakfast?						
· coffee						
· juice						
· milk						
· cereal						
· bread and butter						
· other: _____						
2. What do you do after school?						
· see friends						
· play sports						
· do homework						
· other: _____						
3. What do you do in the evening?						
· use the computer						
· do homework						
· watch TV						
· other: _____						
4. What do you do on weekends?						
· sleep all morning						
· clean my room						
· help around the house						
· other: _____						

12 Practice

A. GROUPS. First, write your country in the chart. Then write the foods you usually have for breakfast.

B. Use the Internet to find out what kinds of food people from other countries have for breakfast.

C. Complete the chart with the information from Exercise B.

D. GROUPS. Discuss the questions.

1. Which countries have similar breakfast foods?
2. Which breakfast foods do you find unique or interesting?
3. Which breakfast foods from other countries have you tried? Which ones would you like to try?

COUNTRY	BREAKFAST
Your country	
Australia	
Japan	
Egypt	
Scotland	
France	
Canada	

13 Reading

A. Study the graph of a teenager's typical day.

A Day in the Life of a Student

HOURS

Sleep 8 School 7 Homework 2 TV 4 Other 3

B. Answer the questions.

1. How many hours a day does the student sleep? _8 hours_
2. How many hours a day does the student spend in school? _____
3. How many hours of homework a day does the student do? _____
4. How many hours of television a day does the student watch? _____

C. Create a bar graph of your typical school day.

Hours

Sleep Do homework Watch TV Play Use computer

14 Speaking

PAIRS. Compare your bar graph with that of your classmate.

For example:

I sleep eight hours a day. You . . .
I do two hours of homework a day. You . . .
I watch three hours of TV a day. You . . .

15 Listening

A. (B16) **Listen to Doris describe her typical day. Then complete the chart.**

Activity	Time
Gets up	6 A.M.
Bus picks her up	
School starts	
School ends	
Gets home	
Eats dinner	
Goes to bed	

B. (B17) **Listen again and complete the sentences.**

When Doris gets home, she always does the following:

1. First, she __looks for something to eat__.

2. Then she _____.

3. After that, she _____.

4. Next, she _____.

5. Finally, she _____.

16 Writing

What's your typical day or week like? Write about it on the paper on the right.

I am always busy on a school day.

I usually get up at six. First,

Progress check   *Units 7 and 8*

Grammar

A. Match the responses with the situations. (1 point each)

1. It's sunny, but the lights are on. __c__

2. Your friend is at your door. _____

3. Your sister is locking the door, but you need to go back in. _____

4. It's raining outside. Your brother's opening the windows. _____

5. Your classmate is talking loudly during class. _____

   a. Don't open the windows.
   b. Be quiet.
   c. Please turn off the lights.
   d. Don't lock the door.
   e. Please come in.

B. Write sentences about what you can and can't do. (3 points each)

1. A language you can or can't speak
   I can speak English.

2. An instrument you can or can't play
   _____

3. An activity you can or can't do
   _____

4. A sport you can or can't play
   _____

C. Insert the frequency adverbs. (1 point each)

1. I visit my grandparents on Sundays. (*always*)
   always

2. We are home on Saturdays. (*usually*)

3. My dad goes out on Friday evenings. (*rarely*)

4. I watch TV on a school day. (*never*)

5. I am busy on weekends. (*sometimes*)

Vocabulary

D. Write the times in words. (3 points each)

1. 9:45 __It's a quarter to ten.__

2. 8:50 _____

3. 4:30 _____

4. 12:25 _____

5. 5:00 _____

E. Write three more things you do when you wake up on a school day. (3 points each)

   I brush my teeth.
   _____
   _____
   _____

Communication

F. Answer the question about your routine. Write four more sentences using sequence words. (3 points per sentence)

   A: What do you usually do when you get home from school?

   B: __First, I have a snack.__
   _____
   _____
   _____
   _____

Now I can . . .
❏ talk about abilities.
❏ ask for permission.
❏ talk about daily routines.

Game 3 Race track

You need:

- a coin
- a game piece for yourself (an eraser, etc.)

Useful language

- Your turn. / My turn!
- That's a good one.
- That's not right. It's . . .
- You win. / I win!

Steps:

1. Begin at "Start" and flip the coin. For heads, move one space. For tails, move two spaces.

2. Follow the rules in the key: Ask questions, say sentences, go back, or go forward. If you make a mistake, go back one space.

3. Then it's the next person's turn.

4. The first person to cross the finish line wins.

Player 1

Player 2

START

sometimes

usually

your family

our teacher

do homework

go to school

go back 1

get up

go forward 1

have

go to bed

has

dance

swim

KEY

- Ask a question.
- Say a sentence.
- Go back 1 space.
- Go forward 1 space.

always

never

go back 1

on weekends

can't stand

FINISH

go forward 1

after school

love

Project 3   *A snapshot of a classmate*

Make an oral presentation about a classmate. Interview a classmate about his or her leisure time. Take notes. Then make a presentation. Use the steps below as a guide.

1. Ask a classmate about his or her leisure time. Then find out about his or her favorite leisure activity. Ask information and *Yes/No* questions to find out as many details as possible.

What do you do in your leisure time?
What's your favorite leisure activity?
When do you usually . . . ?
Who do you usually . . . with?
Where do you usually . . . ?
Do you have a favorite (team, TV show, etc)?
Who's your favorite (player, actor, etc.)?
Why do you like (him or her)?
Do you like . . . ?

2. As you interview your classmate, take short notes on note cards.

- *listens to music, watches TV, plays soccer*
- *loves soccer*
- *usually plays after school, on weekends*
- *usually with friends in his neighborhood*

3. Study your notes and try to remember the information. Then stand and make an oral presentation to your group or class. Try not to look at your notes. Make eye contact and use gestures to make your presentation interesting.

Victor listens to music, watches TV, and plays soccer in his leisure time. He really loves soccer. He usually plays after school and on weekends. He usually plays with friends in his neighborhood. They always play in a park near his house. His favorite soccer team is . . .

1 Reading

B18 **Read along silently as you listen. Underline some of the interesting places and activities in Miami.**

Miami, Florida, is a tourist's paradise. It has a tropical climate and sandy white beaches. Miami is home to many Spanish-speaking immigrants. English and Spanish are the major languages spoken there. It is often called the "Gateway to Latin America."

There are many interesting places to visit in Miami. There's the Metrozoo, the Seaquarium, the Planetarium, the Venetian Pool, and the Vizcaya Museum and Gardens. There are beautiful parks there, too.

South of Miami there's a place called Coconut Grove. If you love shopping or if you enjoy the theater and the arts, Coconut Grove is the place for you. You can go to shows, visit museums, shop at expensive stores, go to dance clubs, or eat at fabulous restaurants.

And, of course, there are some great beaches in Miami, where you can hang out and people-watch, relax in the sun, or go for a swim in the ocean or bay.

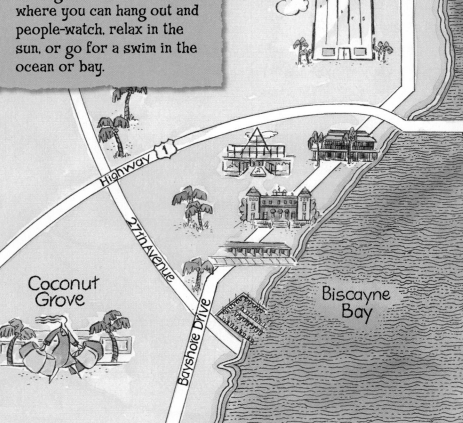

Coral Gables

Coconut Grove

Highway 1

27th Avenue

Bayshore Drive

Biscayne Bay

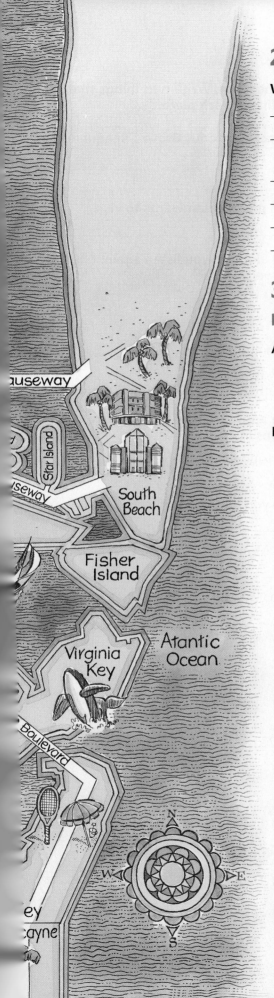

2 Comprehension

Write *True* or *False* before each statement.

_____ **1.** Miami is in Florida, U.S.A.

_____ **2.** Spanish and Portuguese are the two major languages in Miami.

_____ **3.** It is usually cold in Miami.

_____ **4.** You can visit a planetarium in Miami.

_____ **5.** Tourists can go to Coconut Grove to shop.

_____ **6.** Miami doesn't have any beaches.

3 Vocabulary

Places in a town or city

A. B19 Listen and repeat.

- bank
- mall
- restaurant
- bookstore
- movie theater
- supermarket
- bus stop
- museum
- zoo
- drugstore
- post office
- park

B. Match the places with their descriptions.

1. bank _*b*_
2. drugstore _____
3. supermarket _____
4. museum _____
5. post office _____
6. movie theater _____
7. zoo _____
8. bookstore _____
9. park _____
10. restaurant _____
11. mall _____
12. bus stop _____

a. a place with lots of stores and restaurants

b. a place where you save or borrow money

c. a place where you buy and eat food

d. a place where you buy books

e. a place where you watch movies

f. a place where you buy medicine

g. a place where you wait for buses

h. a place where you see artwork and other exhibits

i. a place where you see different kinds of animals

j. a place where you mail letters and packages

k. a place with grass and trees where you can play and relax

l. a place where you shop for food and things for the house

4 Practice

Play a word guessing game! Go to page 132.

5 Dialogue

B20 **Cover the dialogue and listen.**

Andy: So where would you like to go today, Brian?

Brian: I'm not sure. Can I look at the map? Venetian Pool . . . Is this just a pool?

Andy: Not really. There are also waterfalls and restaurants there.

Brian: Let's go there! Where is it?

Andy: It's in Coral Gables, between Coral Way and 40th Street.

Liza: And there's also the Seaquarium.

Andy: Oh, yeah. You can see sharks there.

Brian: Awesome! Can we go there today?

Andy: Sure. You can see dolphins there, too. And then we can go to the Planetarium.

Brian: Great! And what about Coconut Grove? What's that?

Andy: It's Liza's favorite place. It's across from Coral Gables.

Liza: It's a shopping place. There are really great restaurants there, too.

Brian: Umm, I think I'll skip Coconut Grove. I hate malls.

6 Comprehension

A. Look at the chart. Write two things that you can find in each place.

Venetian Pool	Coconut Grove	Seaquarium
waterfalls		

B. Write the places Brian wants to visit.

_____, _____, _____

C. B21 Read along as you listen again. Check your answers.

7 Useful expressions

A. B22 Listen and repeat.

- I'm not sure. • Great!
- Not really. • Oh, yeah.

B. Write the appropriate responses. Use the expressions in Exercise A.

1. **A:** Let's go to the movies.

   B: _____Great!_____

2. **A:** Do you like Tom Cruise?

   B: _____. I prefer Brad Pitt.

3. **A:** It's Mom's birthday today, remember?

   B: _____

4. **A:** What would you like to do today?

   B: _____

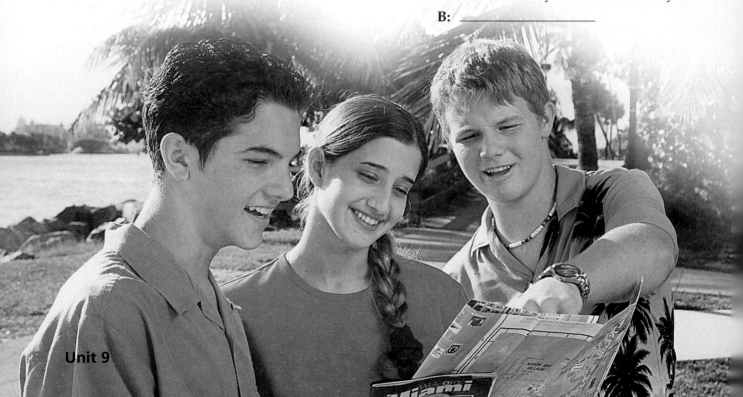

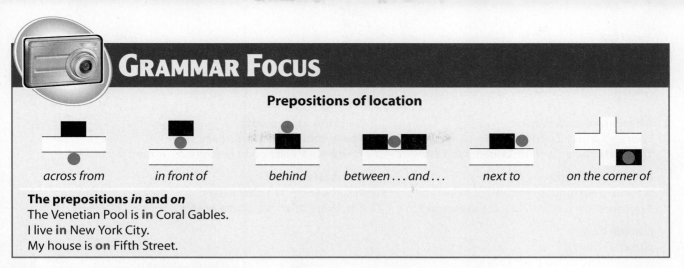

GRAMMAR FOCUS

Prepositions of location

| across from | in front of | behind | between...and... | next to | on the corner of |

The prepositions *in* and *on*
The Venetian Pool is **in** Coral Gables.
I live **in** New York City.
My house is **on** Fifth Street.

Discovering grammar

Look at the pictures in the grammar chart. Circle the correct answers.

1. (*Across from* / *In front of*) means "on the other side."
2. (*Between* / *Behind*) means "at the back of something."
3. (*Between* / *Next to*) means "in the middle of two things."
4. (*On the corner of* / *In front of*) is the point where two streets meet.
5. Use (*in* / *on*) with the name of a street.
6. Use (*in* / *on*) with the name of a place.

Practicing grammar

8 Practice

Look at the map. Complete the sentences with prepositions of location from the grammar chart.

1. The post office is <u>on the corner of</u> Main Street and Third Avenue.
2. The park is _____ the mall and the hotel.
3. The zoo is _____ Main Street.
4. The bus stop is _____ the supermarket.
5. The bookstore is _____ to the drugstore.
6. The bank is _____ the supermarket.

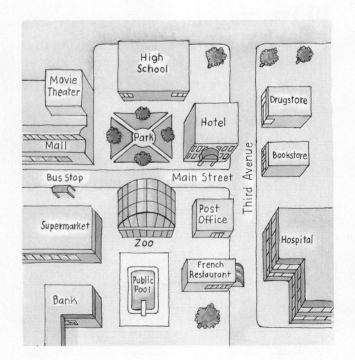

9 Practice

PAIRS. Look at the map again. Take turns. Ask where each place on the map is.

For example:

A: Where's the pool?
B: It's behind the zoo.

GRAMMAR FOCUS

There is/There are

Affirmative statements	**Negative statements**
There's a mall next to the park.	**There isn't** a mall in my town.
There are some good restaurants in Miami.	**There aren't** any good restaurants around my school.
***Yes/No* questions**	**Short answers**
Is there a Portuguese restaurant in Miami?	Yes, **there is**. / No, **there isn't**.
Are there any electronic stores in this mall?	Yes, **there are**. / No, **there aren't**.
Contraction	
There's = There is	

Discovering grammar

Look at the grammar chart. Circle the correct answers.

1. Use a (*singular / plural*) noun after *there is*.
2. Use a (*singular / plural*) noun after *there are*.
3. Use (*some / any*) after *there aren't*.
4. Use (*some / any*) after *are there*.

Practicing grammar

10 Practice

A. **Look at the map. Write sentences using the following:**

- *There is, There are, There isn't any, There aren't any*
- the vocabulary in Exercise 3
- prepositions of location

1. <u>There aren't any banks on the map.</u>
2. <u>There's a zoo across from the YMCA.</u>
3. _____
4. _____
5. _____
6. _____
7. _____
8. _____
9. _____
10. _____

B. **PAIRS. Give your sentences to another student and have him or her check them. Who has the most correct sentences?**

11 Practice

A. **Look at the map carefully. Try to remember the places on it.**

B. **PAIRS. Take turns. Student A, look at your map and ask Student B three *Yes/No* questions about the places on the map. Student B, close your book and answer Student A's questions. Keep score of the correct guesses.**

For example:

A: Is there a mall on the map?
B: Umm . . . Yes, there is!
A: No, there isn't. Next question. Are there . . . ?

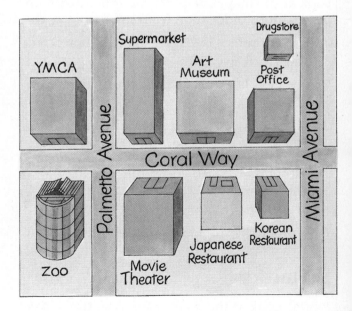

12 Pronunciation

Intonation in *Yes/No* questions and short answers

A. (B23) Listen to the questions and answers. Notice how the voice falls on the last word in the short answers.

Questions

A: Is there a mall in this area?

A: Is there a hotel near the mall?

A: Are there any restaurants near your house?

A: Are there any stores in your neighborhood?

Answers

B: Yes, there is.

B: No, there isn't.

B: Yes, there are.

B: No, there aren't.

B. (B24) Listen again. Then role-play the conversations.

Learn to learn

Prepare before a presentation.

Prepare for speaking activities by writing down some of the things you want to say or ask.

GROUPS. Prepare for part B of Exercise 13 by writing down some of the things you want to say in your presentation. Prepare for part C by writing down some questions.

---

13 Your turn

A. GROUPS. Pretend you're town planners. Your government asks you to plan a new area in your town for teenagers. Follow these instructions:

1. Discuss the places you want to include in your town.
2. Make a sketch of your plan on a big piece of paper. Make your plans colorful and fun.
3. Name your town.

B. GROUPS. Present your town plans to the whole class. Use *There is*, *There are*, and prepositions of location in your presentation.

C. CLASS. Ask the town planners questions about their plans for the town. Ask *Yes/No* and *Where* questions. Give comments about the plans.

For example:

Student 1: Is there a . . . ?
Presenter: No, there isn't a . . ./there aren't any . . .
Student 1: Why not?
Student 2: Excuse me. I think the public pool is very small.

D. Vote on the plan that you like best. Explain your choice.

TEEN TALK

GROUPS. Talk about a favorite vacation place or a favorite place in your town or city. Ask your classmates about their favorite place. Find out where it is and what you can do and see there.

Useful language:
- What's your favorite . . . ?
- What can you do there?
- My favorite place is . . .
- I love it!
- It's awesome there.
- It's in/on . . . (*location*)
- There's/There are . . .
- Let's go there. (*Suggest when to go.*)

14 Vocabulary

Leisure activities

A. Label the pictures with the following:

eat out	go to a party
go shopping	visit grandparents
hang out with friends	watch a DVD

B. Look at Exercise A. Put three checks (✔✔✔) next to the activities you *always* do on weekends; two checks (✔✔) next to the ones you *sometimes* or *often* do on weekends; and an *X* next to the ones you *never* do on weekends.

C. PAIRS. Talk about your weekend activities.

For example:

A: What do you usually do on weekends?
B: Well, I usually go out with my parents. How about you?
A: I sometimes visit my grandparents.

15 Communication

Make suggestions

A. B25 Listen to the conversation.

A: Would you like to go to the movies this weekend?
B: Sorry. I can't. I don't have any money.
A: Oh, OK. Let's watch a DVD at my house then.
B: Good idea!

B. PAIRS. Invite your classmate to do any of the activities in Exercise 14A.

16 Listening

A. B26 Look at the ads as you listen to the conversation. Where do the kids want to go? Circle the ad.

B. B27 Listen again. Circle the events, people, and places mom and the kids talk about.

an outdoor movie	Seaquarium
Rolling Stones concert	Vincent van Gogh
Shakespeare festival	exhibit
Picasso exhibit	Black Eyed Peas
Planetarium	concert

go shopping

Putting it together   *A skateboard contest*

A. **B28** **Look at the pictures and read the conversations. Guess what Andy is saying to Liza and Annie. Write the missing lines. Then listen and see if you guessed correctly.**

1. Look, Annie. There's a skateboard contest at the Lipton Club. Let's go.
   Good idea! I'm hungry. Are there any restaurants there?
   I'm sure there are.

2. Mom, where's the Lipton Club?
   It's on Crandon Boulevard, next to the park.

3. Please understand, Caroline. There's a lot going on at my house.
   But I can't see you every day.

4. Uh-oh. Andy's in trouble again with Caroline.

5. Hey, Andy. Would you like to do something fun?

6. Oh, well, Liza. Let's go get Brian. The skateboard contest sounds really exciting.

B. CLASS. Discuss the questions.

1. Is Caroline upset with Andy? If so, why?
2. What's Andy's explanation?
3. Is Andy a good boyfriend? Explain your answer.

1 Reading

> **Reading skill:** Reading with a purpose
> Before you read, decide what information you will look for.

A. Read the interview for the things that Halldóra says teens do in their leisure time. Underline them.

B. Fill in the Venn diagram with the things Halldóra says teens do in the winter, year-round, and in the summer.

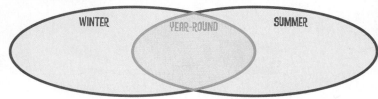

WINTER   YEAR-ROUND   SUMMER

2 Listening

B29 Listen to an interview with Josh Jones, a teen from New York City. Underline the things Josh says teens do in the winter. Circle the things he says teens do in the summer. Circle <u>and</u> underline the things teens do year-round.

go skiing	go out to eat
go to the gym	go ice skating
go shopping	go to movies
go to dance clubs	hang out in the park
go swimming	have picnics
go to museums	go skateboarding

3 Writing

In your notebook, draw a Venn diagram. List the things teens in your city do for fun in the winter, year-round, and in the summer.

4 Speaking

PAIRS. With your partner, discuss the following questions:

1. What do you do for fun in the winter?
2. What do you do for fun in the summer?
3. What do you do for fun year-round?

Teens in Iceland: Hot Pots and Midnight Sun

Teens participate in similar leisure activities all over the world. But each town and country offers some special activities. An interviewer is talking to Halldóra Jónsdóttir, a seventh grader in Reykjavik, Iceland.

Q: What's there to do in Reykjavik, Halldóra?

A: There are lots of things to do, but it depends on the season. We're very far north, and in the winter we get just four hours of sunlight a day.

Q: What do teenagers do for fun in the winter?

A: Well, we do a lot of indoor activities—we read, we watch TV, we go bowling. And we spend a lot of time at the Youth Center. We meet friends there, listen to music, and just hang out.

Q: Do you do any outdoor activities in the winter?

A: Yes, we ski and skate—the ski slopes and skating rinks have lights. And we swim in the hot pots!

Q: Hots pots?!

A: Yes, hot water swimming pools that are outdoors. Reykjavik has a lot of hot springs, and we use the hot water to generate energy. After that, the water goes to heat our homes, and it also goes into hot water pools. So we can swim outside year-round—even when it's snowing. In Reykjavik, there is a famous pool called the Blue Lagoon. The white mud in the pool is very good for your skin.

Q: What's summer like in Reykjavik? Do you mostly stay indoors?

A: No way! In the summer, we have the midnight sun. We get sunlight for 18 hours a day and the sun never really sets. So we spend a lot of time outdoors! We go hiking and camping, and stay up very late!

What's Brian doing?

1 Dialogue

B30 **Cover the dialogue and listen.**

Liza: Where's Brian?
Andy: He's upstairs in the bedroom.
Liza: What's he doing? Is he reading?
Andy: No, he isn't. He's writing an e-mail.
Liza: Who's he writing to? Is he e-mailing his parents?
Andy: I don't know, Liza. Stop bothering me. I'm watching TV.
Liza: I'm just asking you questions.
Andy: I know, but you're bothering me.
Liza: Gee, Andy. You're grumpy today. I'm out of here.

Learning goals

Communication
  Ask what someone's doing now
  Describe what's happening
    right now
  Talk about a house

Grammar
  The present continuous: *be*
    (*am/is/are*) + verb *-ing*

Vocabulary
  Rooms and parts of a house

2 Comprehension

A. **Cross out the wrong information in each sentence.**
  Then correct it.

  1. Liza is asking about ~~Robbie~~. *Brian*
  2. Andy doesn't know where Brian is.
  3. Brian is reading.
  4. Andy wants to talk to Liza.
  5. Liza says Andy is nice.

B. **B31** **Check your answers. Read along as you listen again.**

3 Useful expressions

B32 **Listen and repeat. Match the expressions with similar meanings.**

1. I don't know. ___b___
2. Stop bothering me. _____
3. You're grumpy. _____
4. I'm out of here. _____

a. I'm leaving right now.
b. I have no idea.
c. Don't ask me a lot of questions.
d. You're in a bad mood.

TEEN TALK

PAIRS. Talk about your favorite place in your house.

Useful language:
• What's your favorite place in your house?
• Why is it your favorite?
• What's in that room?
• Sounds awesome/cool.
• Me, too!
• No way!
• Really?

4 Vocabulary

Rooms and parts of a house

A. **B33 Listen and repeat.**

1. bathroom
2. bedroom
3. dining room
4. garage
5. kitchen
6. living room
7. stairs
8. downstairs
9. upstairs

B. **Label the parts of the house. Use the numbers in Exercise A as your labels.**

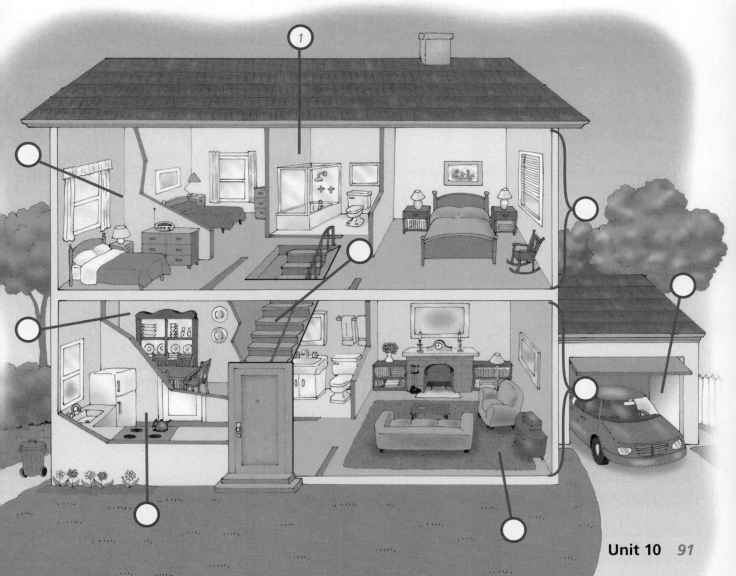

GRAMMAR FOCUS

The present continuous:
be (am/is/are) + verb *-ing*

Affirmative statements		Negative statements	
I'm You're He's She's	} studying.	I'm not You're not He's not She's not	} playing.
You're We're They're	} studying.	You're not We're not They're not	} playing.

Spelling of *-ing* verbs

listen—listen**ing** play—play**ing**
smile—smil**ing**   sit—sit**ting**

Discovering grammar

Look at the grammar chart. Complete
the rules.

1. Use _____ + verb *-ing* with *I*.
   a. am **b.** is **c.** are

2. Use _____ + verb *-ing* with *He, She,*
   and *It*.
   a. am **b.** is **c.** are

3. Use _____ + verb *-ing* with *We, You,*
   and *They*.
   a. am **b.** is **c.** are

Practicing grammar

5 Practice

Write the *-ing* forms. Follow the patterns.

Group 1: Add *-ing*.

1. play → *playing*   3. fix → _____
2. study → _____   4. show → _____

Group 2: Drop the *-e*.

1. write → *writing*   3. leave → _____
2. use → _____   4. make → _____

Group 3: Double the consonant.

1. plan → *planning*   3. shop → _____
2. run → _____   4. get → _____

6 Practice

Complete the sentences with the present
continuous form of the verbs in parentheses.

1. Liza and Andy ___*are talking*___. (*talk*)
2. Andy _____ TV. (*watch*)
3. Liza _____ Andy questions. (*ask*)
4. Andy _____ annoyed. (*get*)
5. Brian _____ in front of the
   computer. (*sit*)
6. He _____. (*not read*)
7. He _____ to his parents. (*write*)

7 Practice

What are the people in the pictures doing?

1. she/use her computer _____
2. he/take a shower _____
3. she/do homework _____
4. they/play tennis _____

8 Practice

A. Complete Brian's e-mail with the present continuous form of the verbs in parentheses. Use contractions where possible.

B. Make two sentences. In the first sentence, correct the wrong information. In the second sentence, give the correct information.

1. Brian is sharing Robbie's bedroom.

   Brian isn't sharing Robbie's bedroom.

   He's sharing Andy's bedroom.

2. Mr. and Mrs. Gibson are working in the garden.

   _____

   _____

3. Robbie is helping Andy with dinner.

   _____

   _____

4. Andy and Liza are helping their parents.

   _____

   _____

5. Brian is doing his homework.

   _____

   _____

Hi, Mom and Dad. How's everything at home? (**1.** *I/have*) ___I'm having___ a wonderful time here. (**2.** *I/enjoy*) _____ Miami a lot. It's a great place! Are you planning to visit me? You could stay at the Gibsons' house during your visit.

The house has four bedrooms. (**3.** *I/share*) _____ Andy's bedroom. Andy and I are great friends. He lets me use his things, including his computer. (**4.** *I/use*) _____ his computer right now.

It's almost dinnertime here. (**5.** *Mr. and Mrs. Gibson/prepare*) _____ dinner. (**6.** *Robbie/help*) _____ his parents. (**7.** *Andy and Liza/watch*) _____ TV in the living room. I know, Mom. You're wondering why (**8.** *we/not help*) _____ with dinner. Well, Andy, Liza, and I always do the dishes afterwards.

I'm attaching a picture of me. (**9.** *I/stand*) _____ in front of the Gibson's house. Looks great, right? I mean the house, not me.

GRAMMAR FOCUS

The present continuous tense: *be (am/is/are)* + verb *–ing*

Yes/No questions	Affirmative answers	Negative answers
Am I Are you Is he Is she } **studying?**	Yes, you **are**. Yes, I **am**. Yes, he **is**. Yes, she **is**.	No, you're **not**. / No, you **aren't**. No, **I'm not**. No, he's **not**. / No, he **isn't**. No, she's **not**. / No, she **isn't**.
Are you Are we Are they } **studying?**	Yes, we **are**. Yes, we/you **are**. Yes, they **are**.	No, we're **not**. / No, we **aren't**. No, we're/you're **not**. / No, we/you **aren't**. No, they're **not**. / No, they **aren't**.

Information questions	Short answers	Long answers
What **are** you **doing?**	Studying.	**I'm studying**.
What's she/he **doing?**	Watching TV.	She's/He's **watching** TV.
What **are** they **doing?**	Doing homework.	They're **doing** homework.

Discovering grammar

Look at the grammar chart. Answer the questions.

1. What comes first in present continuous *Yes/No* questions? _____

2. What comes first in present continuous information questions? _____

3. Can you contract *am* + *not*? _____

Practicing grammar

9 Practice

A. **PAIRS.** Look at the picture. Try to remember what each person is doing.

B. PAIRS. Student A, close your book. Student B, ask *Yes/No* questions about the picture. Use the cues. Then switch roles.

For example:

A: Is Ms. Simpson singing?
B: No, she's not.
A: What's she doing?
B: She's teaching.

1. Wendy, Tracy, and Daniel / take notes
2. Brad / listen to Mrs. Simpson
3. Jen and Angie / play
4. Jessica / talk on her cell phone

10 Your turn

PAIRS. Take turns. Ask what three people around you are doing.

For example:

A: What's Dylan doing?
B: He's reading a text message. How about . . . ?
A: They're talking.

11 Practice

Have a competition! Go to page 133.

12 Pronunciation

Stress on important words

A. B34 Listen and repeat.

A: **What** are you **do**ing?
B: I'm **stu**dying.
A: **What** are they **do**ing?
B: They're **do**ing their **home**work.

B. PAIRS. Practice the conversations.

13 Communication

Ask what someone's doing now

A. B35 Listen to the conversation.

Liza: Hello.
Annie: Hi, Liza. What are you doing right now?
Liza: Watching TV in my room. Why?

Annie: I'm bored. Are Brian and Andy doing anything?
Liza: No. Would you like to come over?
Annie: OK.

B. PAIRS. Role-play. Imagine you are at home after school. Have a phone conversation like the one in Exercise A.

14 Writing

PAIRS. It's the weekend. Write instant messages between you and a classmate. Talk about what you're doing and what's going on.

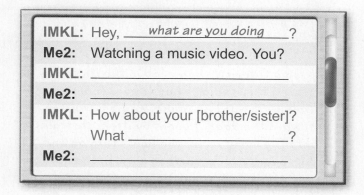

IMKL: Hey, ____*what are you doing*____?
Me2: Watching a music video. You?
IMKL: _____
Me2: _____
IMKL: How about your [brother/sister]? What _____?
Me2: _____

15 Listening

A. B36 Listen to the interview. Circle the two new inventions the scientists are working on to help the environment.

a. a robot that cleans your room
b. a robot that makes clothes
c. a robot that eats garbage
d. a machine that cooks your meals
e. a machine that washes dishes without water

B. Which of these things are important to George Getty? Circle the letters.

a. the environment
b. making a lot of money
c. saving energy
d. making beautiful machines
e. saving water
f. stopping pollution

16 Reading

A. Look at the title and the pictures in the article below. What do you expect to read about? Circle all that apply.

   a. a family with intelligent children
   b. a beautifully decorated home
   c. a high-tech home
   d. high-tech appliances
   e. the high cost of houses
   f. life in the United States

B. **B37** Read along silently as you listen.

INTELLIGENT HOMES OF THE FUTURE

In a futuristic home lab in the United States, this is what's happening: A man is walking toward his house. As he is walking toward the door, it opens by itself. He walks into the living room; the lights turn on and his favorite song starts to play. In the garage, one of his cars is making an appointment with the mechanic. The man goes to the kitchen and stops in front of the refrigerator. It is printing out a shopping list. Science fiction? No. Everything is real! In this home lab, engineers are developing intelligent refrigerators, lamps, TV sets, and cars.

Some homeowners are already testing these intelligent appliances. In Virginia, some residents can check that the doors are locked from their offices. In Boston, some homeowners are using intelligent ovens. They put food in the oven before going to bed. Then they program the oven to refrigerate and cook the food for the next day.

In the future, an intelligent house can turn up the heat in the bedroom fifteen minutes before the homeowner wakes up, turn on the bedroom light when the alarm clock sounds, and turn on the coffee maker. The house can also display the news on the video screen in the bathroom and turn on the shower. The bathroom scale is very intelligent, too. If the homeowner is putting on weight, it can change the homeowner's menu. Now that's pretty cool.

17 Comprehension

1. Write what each of these things in the futuristic home lab can do.

   a. the door _It can open by itself._

   b. the refrigerator _____

   c. the car _____

   d. the oven _____

2. In the future, what can a bathroom scale do?

_____

18 Speaking

PAIRS. **Close your books and see how much you can remember. Answer this question: What can an intelligent home do?**

For example:

A: The door can open by itself.
B: The lights . . .

Progress check

Units 9 and 10

> **Test-taking tip:** Work carefully.
> Work slowly enough and carefully so you don't make careless errors.

Grammar

A. Look at the street map and answer the questions. Use the cues. (2 points each)

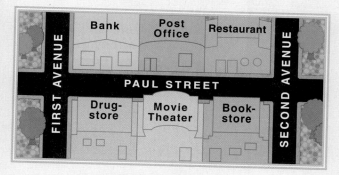

1. Where's the restaurant? *(next to)*
   <u>The restaurant is next to the post office.</u>

2. Where's the movie theater? *(between . . . and)*
   _____

3. Where's the bank? *(across from)*
   _____

4. Where's the drugstore? *(on the corner of)*
   _____

B. Look at the map again. Complete the sentences with *There is a/There isn't a* or *There are/There aren't any.* (2 points each)

1. <u>There aren't any</u> cars on the streets.
2. _____ restaurant on the corner of Paul Street and Second Avenue.
3. _____ houses in the area.
4. _____ bookstore on Paul Street.
5. _____ bank on Second Avenue.

C. Complete the paragraph with the present continuous. (2 points each)

It's a nice day. The sun (**1.** *shine*) <u>is shining</u>, and I (**2.** *sit*) _____ on a bench in the park. I (**3.** *read*) _____ a book. Some people (**4.** *walk*) _____ their dogs. Kids (**5.** *play*) _____ soccer. A man and a woman (**6.** *jog*) _____.

D. Ask information questions about the underlined words. (3 points each)

1. I am sitting <u>on a bench in the park</u>.
   (Where) ___<u>Where are you sitting?</u>___

2. I am reading a <u>book</u>.
   (What) _____

3. The kids are playing <u>soccer</u>.
   (What) _____

4. <u>A woman</u> is jogging.
   (Who) _____

5. The old man is sleeping <u>on the grass</u>.
   (Where) _____

Vocabulary

E. Match the places with the objects. (1 point each)

1. drugstore
2. museum
3. bookstore
4. post office
5. movie theater
6. supermarket

a. books and magazines
b. medicine
c. *Spider-Man*, popcorn
d. letters, stamps
e. fruits and vegetables
f. paintings, exhibits

Communication

F. Complete the conversation. (3 points each)

A: _____
B: Nothing much. I'm watching TV. Why?
A: _____
B: A volleyball game? _____
   Where is it?
A: At the park, next to the police station.

> **Now I can . . .**
> ❏ make suggestions.
> ❏ talk about leisure activities.
> ❏ explain what's happening now.

11 Did he call her again today?

1 Dialogue

B38 Cover the dialogue and listen.

Liza: Andy, where's Brian?
Andy: I don't know.
Robbie: He's in the house. He's on the phone.
Liza: With Joey? Did he call her again today?
Robbie: No. Joey's not home.
Liza: Good. Listen, let's have a surprise party for Brian.
Andy: That's a great idea, Liza!
Robbie: Yeah! And we can invite Joey because Brian likes her.
Liza: What? Did he say that?
Robbie: No, he didn't. But they talked on the phone all day yesterday. And they shopped together, too.
Andy: Don't gossip, Robbie. That's not very nice. When do you want to have the party, Liza?
Liza: The twenty-sixth.
Andy: OK. Hey, let's have a costume party!
Liza: Excellent idea, Andy.

2 Comprehension

A. Answer the questions.

1. Who's looking for Brian?
2. Where's Brian?
3. What does Liza suggest for Brian?
4. When does she want to have the party?
5. What kind of party does Andy suggest?

B. B39 Read along as you listen again. Check your answers.

3 Useful expressions

A. (B40) **Listen and repeat. Draw a smiley (☺) next to the expressions of approval and a frownie (☹) next to those that express disapproval.**

- That's a great idea. ☺
- Don't gossip. _____
- That's not very nice. _____
- Excellent idea. _____

B. **PAIRS. Complete the conversation with expressions from Exercise A. Then role-play the conversation.**

A: What a beautiful day! Let's sit outside.

B: _That's a great idea._

A: Look. There's Zack and Dana. I think Zack likes Dana, but Dana doesn't like him.

B: _____. _____.

A: Sorry.

4 Vocabulary

Past time expressions

A. (B41) **Listen and repeat.**

- yesterday
- last night
- last week
- last month

- last year
- last Monday
- a few minutes ago
- three days ago

- a week ago
- a month ago
- a year ago

B. **Look at the calendars. Write the dates, days, or months next to the expressions.**

1. yesterday _January 16th_
2. last night _____
3. last week _____
4. last month _____

5. last Wednesday _____
6. three days ago _____
7. a week ago _____
8. a month ago _____

GRAMMAR FOCUS

The simple past of regular verbs

Affirmative statements
I **talked** to him yesterday.
She **smiled** at him.
He **stopped** by a few minutes ago.
We **cried** because they moved away.

Negative statements
I **didn't talk** to him.
He **didn't smile** back.
He **didn't stop** for long.
They **didn't cry** at all.

Contractions
didn't = did not

Discovering grammar

Look at the grammar chart. Complete the grammar rules with expressions from the box.

-d	simple past	ago	*stop*
-ed	yesterday	last	base

1. Use the _____ to talk about actions that are finished.

2. _____, _____, and _____ are past time expressions.

3. The base form of *stopped* is _____.

4. To form the simple past of regular verbs in affirmative statements, add _____ or _____ to the base form of a verb.

5. To form the simple past of verbs in negative statements, use *did + not +* the _____ form of a main verb.

Practicing grammar

5 Practice

Have a competition! Go to page 133.

6 Practice

Complete the sentences with the simple past.

1. Liza (*ask*) ___asked___ about Brian a while ago.
2. Andy and Robbie (*play*) _____ basketball in the yard this morning.
3. Brian (*stop by*) _____ five minutes ago.
4. He (*try*) _____ to call Joey an hour ago.
5. Liza (*worry*) _____ that Brian called Joey again.
6. Brian and Joey (*enjoy*) _____ shopping together yesterday.
7. Liza (*suggest*) _____ a party for Brian.

7 Practice

A. **Write a summary of the conversation on page 98. Use the simple past of the verbs in the box.**

agree	plan	stop
ask	play	suggest

This morning, Andy and Robbie played basketball
in the yard. Brian stopped by for a few minutes.
Liza _____

_____
She _____

_____
Andy _____

_____
They _____

_____

B. **PAIRS. Read your classmate's summary. Circle any incorrect information or incorrect use of the simple past. Correct the errors in your stories together.**

TEEN TALK

GROUPS. Liza is not happy because Brian seems to like Joey. Liza feels jealous of Joey. Talk about situations when people get jealous.

Useful language:
- What situations can make people jealous?
- Can you give an example?
- Do you think it's natural to feel jealous sometimes?
- Do you get jealous?
- Sometimes.
- Of course.
- I'm sometimes a little jealous of my brother/ sister.
- Do you talk to your parents about it?
- Why not?

8 Pronunciation

The pronunciation of -d and -ed endings

A. **B42** **Listen and repeat.**

/t/	/d/	/əd/
stopped	enjoyed	suggested
asked	played	wanted
talked	tried	decided

B. **B43** **Listen. Circle the verbs that end with the /t/ sound.**

1. I (stopped) and listened to the music.
2. They talked while they played.
3. She laughed when he tried to kiss her.
4. We stayed home and watched a video.

Learn to learn

Take notes in class.

Taking notes in class helps you understand your lessons.

Here are some note-taking tips:
1. Don't try to write down every word you hear.
2. Listen for answers to *who, where, when,* and *what* questions.

For example:

1. Who: _Andy____, _____, _____
2. What: _cake____, _____, _____,
   _____, _____, _____
3. When/What time: _before 4_, _____

9 Listening

B44 **Listen to Caroline's message for Andy. Circle the correct answers.**

1. What did Caroline order for the party?
   (ice cream)   (cake)
   cookies   sandwiches
2. How many kinds of ice cream did she order?
   one   two   three   four
3. Who cooked for the party?
   Caroline   Caroline's mom
   Liza   Liza's mom
4. What did she cook for the party?
   hot dogs   hamburgers   spaghetti   cake
5. What did Caroline ask Andy to pick up from the supermarket?
   lemonade   candy
   peanuts   ice cream
6. When is Caroline going to Andy's house?
   at two o'clock   at three o'clock
   at four o'clock   at five o'clock

GRAMMAR FOCUS

The simple past of regular verbs

Yes/No questions	Short answers
Did you **talk** to Brian yesterday?	Yes, I **did**. / No, I **didn't**.
Did he **stop** by a few minutes ago?	Yes, he **did**. / No, he **didn't**.
Did you **cry** last night?	Yes, we **did**. / No, we **didn't**.

Discovering grammar

Look at the grammar chart. Circle the correct answers.

1. *Yes/No* questions begin with (*did / do*).
2. (*Add / Do not add*) *-d* or *-ed* to the main verbs in simple past questions.

Practicing grammar

10 Practice

A. **Write *Yes/No* questions. Use the simple past and the cues.**

1. finish your homework last night

   _____

2. watch a movie last Saturday

   _____

3. call your parents this morning

   _____

4. like the last Harry Potter movie

   _____

5. clean your room last weekend

   _____

6. text your friends yesterday

   _____

B. **PAIRS. Take turns. Ask and answer the questions in Exercise A.**

For example:

A: Did you finish your homework last night?
B: Yes, I did. How about you?
A: No, I didn't.

11 Practice

A. **PAIRS. Complete the questionnaire for yourself. Put a check (✔) next to the ones you did and an *X* next to the ones you didn't do. Then ask a classmate the questions.**

What kind of a person are you?

1 HOW HELPFUL ARE YOU?

Yesterday, did you . . .   Me You
• help clean the house? ☐ ☐
• wash the dishes after eating? ☐ ☐
• clean your room? ☐ ☐
• organize your things in your room? ☐ ☐

2 HOW STUDIOUS ARE YOU?

Last night, did you . . .   Me You
• finish your homework? ☐ ☐
• study for your tests? ☐ ☐
• prepare your things for the next day? ☐ ☐

3 HOW SOCIABLE ARE YOU?

Last weekend, did you . . .   Me You
• watch a movie with friends? ☐ ☐
• invite friends over to your house? ☐ ☐
• call your friends? ☐ ☐
• stop by a friend's house? ☐ ☐

4 HOW HEALTHY ARE YOU?

Last weekend, did you . . .   Me You
• exercise? ☐ ☐
• walk a lot? ☐ ☐
• play any sport? ☐ ☐
• avoid sweets and junk food? ☐ ☐

B. **GROUPS. Join another pair. Compare your answers. Who is . . .**

a. helpful? _____

b. studious? _____

c. sociable? _____

d. healthy? _____

GRAMMAR FOCUS

The simple past of regular verbs

Information questions	Short answers	Long answers
Who **did** your sister **call** this morning?	Me.	My sister **called** me this morning.
When **did** you **talk** to Brian?	Yesterday.	I **talked** to him yesterday.
What time **did** he **stop** by?	A few minutes ago.	He **stopped** by a few minutes ago.
Why **did** you **cry**?	Because my mom **yelled** at me.	I **cried** because my mom **yelled** at me.
With *Who* as subject		
Who **called** you this morning?	My sister.	My sister **called** me this morning.

Discovering grammar

Look at the grammar chart. Circle the correct answers.

1. When you use *did* with a main verb, (*add* -ed / *do not add* -ed) to the main verb.

2. When the subject is *Who*, (*use* / *don't use*) *did* with the main verb.

Practicing grammar

12 Practice

A. Write information questions using the cues.

1. When / last exercise

   <u>When did you last exercise?</u>

2. What time finish studying / last night

   _____

3. What movie / watch / last Saturday

   _____

4. Where / study / yesterday

   _____

5. When / last clean / your room

   _____

6. Why / call / me / last night

   _____

B. **PAIRS.** Student A, ask your classmate questions 1–3 in Exercise A. Student B, answer them.

C. **PAIRS.** Student B, it's your turn. Ask questions 4–6. Student A, answer them.

13 Practice

Write information questions for the underlined words in each sentence.

1. <u>Andy</u> picked up some snacks.

   (Who) <u>Who picked up some snacks ?</u>

2. Andy invited <u>Joey</u> to the party.

   (Who) _____

3. Brian arrived in Miami <u>two months ago</u>.

   (When) _____

4. Liza suggested a party for Brian <u>because he's leaving</u>.

   (Why) _____

5. <u>Brian</u> e-mailed his parents a few days ago.

   (Who) _____

6. Annie called Liza <u>at 10:00</u> this morning.

   (What time) _____

14 Communication

Talk about past events

A. (B45) **Listen to the conversation.**

A: Did you watch *American Idol* last night?
B: No, I didn't. Did you?
A: Yeah. I didn't like it at all.
B: I'm glad I didn't watch it.

B. Talk about what you did last weekend.

15 Reading

Read the instant messages between Liza and Annie. What do the acronyms *B4N* and *TTYL* mean?

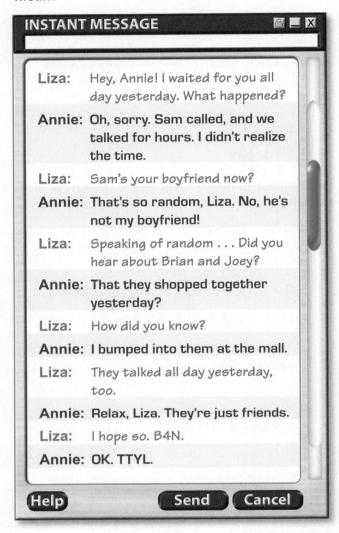

INSTANT MESSAGE

Liza: Hey, Annie! I waited for you all day yesterday. What happened?

Annie: Oh, sorry. Sam called, and we talked for hours. I didn't realize the time.

Liza: Sam's your boyfriend now?

Annie: That's so random, Liza. No, he's not my boyfriend!

Liza: Speaking of random . . . Did you hear about Brian and Joey?

Annie: That they shopped together yesterday?

Liza: How did you know?

Annie: I bumped into them at the mall.

Liza: They talked all day yesterday, too.

Annie: Relax, Liza. They're just friends.

Liza: I hope so. B4N.

Annie: OK. TTYL.

Help   Send   Cancel

16 Comprehension

PAIRS. Draw a smiley (☺) or a frownie (☹) to show how each character felt when she wrote each of these sentences.

1. **Liza:** I waited for you all day yesterday.
   ☹

2. **Annie:** Oh, sorry. ____

3. **Annie:** Sam called. ____

4. **Liza:** They talked all day yesterday, too.
   ____

17 Vocabulary

Emoticons and acronyms

A. **Match the emoticons with the emotions and actions they express.**

Emoticons	Emotions
1. ;-) 😊	a. I'm sad.
2. :-(☹	b. I'm angry.
3. :-) ☺	c. That's funny.
4. :-o 😮	d. I'm joking.
5. >:-< 😠	e. I'm happy.
6. :-D 😃	f. I'm crying.
7. :'(😢	g. I'm surprised.

B. **Match the acronyms with the expressions.**

1. ASAP	a. See you later.
2. B4N	b. Parents are watching.
3. BRB	c. Talk to you later.
4. CUL8R	d. Got to go.
5. G2G	e. As soon as possible.
6. PAW	f. Bye for now.
7. TTYL	g. Be right back.

18 Your turn

GROUPS. Put together a list of emoticons that teenagers like to use. Include what each one means. Share your list with the class.

http://www.teentime.com

TEEN TIME

Putting it together   At the costume party

A. B46 **First, look at the pictures and identify some of the costumes. Then listen and read.**

1. What a great party, Liza! Did you plan all this? Hey, what's wrong?

You know what's wrong, Joey. Brian likes you. And you like him, too.

2. What are you talking about? Brian and I are just good friends.

Why did he call you yesterday? He called you today, too. You know what? He calls you every day!

See what I mean? He likes talking to you. Robbie said you shopped together, too.

Yeah, but we just talk.

You're wrong about Brian and me.

ro! Juliet! Robin od! They just ounced the winner best costume. I nk it's me! Come on.

OK, Superman. We're coming.

5. Oh, no!

B. **CLASS.** **Discuss this question:** Why does Liza say, "Oh, no!"

Unit 11   *105*

Game 4 Add up the questions

You need:

- a die, or write the numbers 1–6 on pieces of paper and fold them up
- a game piece for yourself (an eraser, etc.)

Steps:

1. Work in pairs or small groups.

2. Put your markers on square *a*. Player A reads the sentence aloud. (*Sherri studied Spanish on the stairs last Saturday.*) Player A then rolls the die or picks a folded piece of paper. If the player gets a number from 1–5, he or she asks a question using the question word in that box. (For example, Player A gets a 1: *Who studied Spanish on the stairs last Saturday?*)

3. If Player A asks the question correctly, he or she moves to the next square. Then it's Player B's turn to read the sentence in square *a* and roll the die.

4. If a player rolls a 6, or doesn't ask the question correctly, he or she cannot move to the next square.

5. The first player to complete square *f* wins.

Ask *Who*	Ask *What*	Ask *Where*	Ask *When*	Ask *Did*	Lose a turn

a Sherri studied Spanish on the stairs last Saturday.

b Paco played the piano at a party a few days ago.

c Jerry tried sushi at a Japanese restaurant last June.

d Cathy washed her brother's car on the corner last Sunday.

e Mark watched a magic show at the mall on Monday.

f Kim cooked Korean food in her cooking class two weeks ago.

Project 4 — *A snapshot of a field trip*

Imagine your teacher wants your ideas on a field trip. Think of a place you'd like to visit with your class. Post your suggestion on an Internet message board—or write it on a piece of paper to share with the class. Choose photos to go with your post. Use the message and steps below as a guide.

http://www.pearsoned.com

1. Write your screen name and greet your classmates. Introduce your field trip idea.

SmartTim writes:

Hey everybody! ☺ Let's go on a field trip to the National Aquarium in Baltimore! It's not far from Washington, and it's way cool!

2. Write about the things you can see and do there.

The National Aquarium has over 500 different fish and animals. They have huge fish tanks. You really feel like you're under water. They have lots of sharks, of course. And there are snakes and dolphins, too. In fact, we can see a dolphin show there! And right now there's a special exhibit on frogs. They have some great poison frogs, including an awesome blue poison dart frog.

3. Write about something special your class can see or do.

The aquarium has some great special tours. The best is "Sleepover with the Sharks." Does that sound cool? ;-) We can learn all about sharks and sleep right next to the shark tank! Breakfast is included!

4. Explain where the place is and how to get there. Ask your classmates to reply, and then sign off.

The aquarium is in Baltimore. To get there, we can take the train from Union Station. It just takes about 40 minutes. Then we can take a bus to the aquarium. It's right next to the Inner Harbor, on the water. Sound good? Let me know! G2G! B4N!

5. Let your classmates post replies to your message.

TopCat writes:

Hey SmartTim! Your idea sounds great! Especially the "Sleepover with the Sharks"!! :-o

1 Dialogue

B47 **Cover the dialogue and listen.**

Brian: Good-bye, Mrs. Gibson. Thanks for having me this summer. I really had a great time.

Mom: We're glad you came, Brian. It was fun for us, too. And you were so good with Robbie. Say hi to your parents.

Robbie: Uh, Brian. You can have my baseball. It's my present for you.

Brian: Thank you, Robbie. I left something for you in your room.

Joey: And this is from all of us. It's the family picture you took at the picnic.

Brian: You're a great friend, Joey. Andy, you're cool. Thanks, man.

Andy: No problem, dude. Good luck.

Liza: We'll miss you, Brian. Keep in touch.

Brian: OK. Oh, I almost forgot. This is for you, Liza. Joey thought you'd love this.

Liza: Oh, thank you! It's beautiful.

Brian: Bye, everyone.

All: Bye. Have a great trip. Take care.

Learning goals

Communication
Talk about the past
Say good-bye
Talk about occupations

Grammar
The simple past of *be* (*was/were*)
The simple past of irregular verbs

Vocabulary
Some occupations

2 Comprehension

A. Answer the questions orally.

1. What's special about today?
   Brian is going back to Australia.
2. What is Robbie's present for Brian?
3. Where is Brian's present for Robbie?
4. What is the family's present for Brian?
5. Who helped Brian choose a present for Liza?

B. (B48) **Read along as you listen again. Check your answers.**

3 Useful expressions

A. (B49) **Listen and repeat.**

1. Good-bye./Bye. ___*Bye.*___
2. Thanks for having me. _____
3. Good luck. _____
4. Keep in touch. _____
5. Have a great trip. _____
6. Take care. _____

B. Write these responses next to the appropriate expressions in Exercise A.

a. Thanks.   d. Bye.
b. OK.   e. No problem.
c. You, too.

Learn to learn

Keep a list of everyday words and expressions.

Keeping a list of everyday words and expressions is a good way to increase your vocabulary.

A. PAIRS. List the expressions for greeting and meeting people and for saying good-bye that you've learned in this book.

Meeting and greeting people	Saying good-bye
Hi.	*Take care.*

B. PAIRS. Take turns saying the expressions and responding to them.

Tip: When you greet and say good-bye to your teacher and to each other, use the expressions on your list.

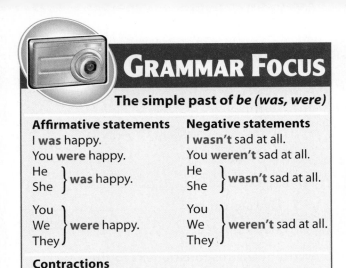

GRAMMAR FOCUS

The simple past of *be (was, were)*

Affirmative statements	Negative statements
I **was** happy.	I **wasn't** sad at all.
You **were** happy.	You **weren't** sad at all.
He She } **was** happy.	He She } **wasn't** sad at all.
You We They } **were** happy.	You We They } **weren't** sad at all.

Contractions	
wasn't = was not	weren't = were not

Discovering grammar

Look at the grammar chart. Complete the rules with words from the box.

was	wasn't	be	were	weren't

1. The simple past forms of _____ are *was* and *were*.

2. Use _____ and _____ with *He*, *She*, and *It*.

3. Use _____ and _____ with *I*, *You*, *We*, and *They*.

Practicing grammar

4 Practice

Complete the sentences with *was*, *wasn't*, *were*, or *weren't*.

Last Saturday, I (1) __was__ at a friend's party. Some of my classmates (2) _____ there, too. The party (3) _____ a lot of fun. The food (4) _____ great. There (5) _____ cakes, cookies, and lots of ice cream! Yum! There (6) _____ games and lots of fun activities. But there (7) _____ any music. There (8) _____ any dancing either. But it (9) _____ a lot of fun because the games (10) _____ awesome.

5 Practice

A. PAIRS. Match the labels with the pictures.

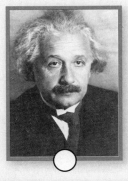

1. the Beatles/(Great Britain) pop and rock group
2. Thomas Edison/(United States) inventor
3. Frida Kahlo and Diego Rivera/(Mexico) painters
4. Albert Einstein/(Germany) scientist
5. Pierre and Marie Curie/(France) scientists
6. Mother Teresa/(Yugoslavia) nun

B. PAIRS. Take turns. Say who the people in the pictures were.

For example:

A: Frida Kahlo and Diego Rivera were Mexican painters.

B: Albert Einstein . . .

GRAMMAR FOCUS

The simple past of be (was/were)

Yes/No questions	Affirmative answers	Negative answers
Was I sad **Were** you sad **Was** he/she sad **Were** we sad **Were** you sad **Were** they sad } to see him go?	Yes, you **were**. Yes, I **was**. Yes, he/she **was**. Yes, we/you **were**. Yes, we **were**. Yes, they **were**.	No, you **weren't**. No, I **wasn't**. No, he/she **wasn't**. No, we/you **weren't**. No, we **weren't**. No, they **weren't**.
Information questions	**Short answers**	**Long answers**
Who **was** at the door? Where **were** you last week? Why **were** they absent? What time **was** your appointment?	Brian. On vacation. Because they **were** sick. At 10:00.	Brian **was** at the door. I **was** on vacation. They **were** absent because they **were** sick. My appointment **was** at 10:00.

Discovering grammar

Look at the grammar chart. Circle the correct answers.

1. In *Yes/No* questions, *was* and *were* come (*before* / *after*) the subject.
2. In information questions, *was* and *were* come (*before* / *after*) the question word.

Practicing grammar

6 Practice

A. Answer the questions about some members of your family.

1. Where were you yesterday at 5:00 P.M.?
   I was at a friend's house.

2. Where were you last Saturday?
   _____

3. Where was your dad last night?
   _____

4. Where was your mom last Saturday?
   _____

5. Where were your grandparents last Sunday?
   _____

6. Where were some of your cousins last weekend?
   _____

B. PAIRS. Try to guess where your classmate and his or her family were by asking *Yes/No* questions about the information in Exercise A.

For example:

A: Were you at school yesterday at 5:00 P.M.?
B: No, I wasn't.
A: Were you at home?
B: No, I wasn't.
A: Were you at a friend's house?
B: Yes, I was!

> You get three points if you guess correctly on the first try, two points on the second try, and one point on the final try. If you're unable to guess correctly after three tries, ask "Where were you/they?" or "Where was he/she?"

7 Pronunciation

The pronunciation of *was* and *were*

A. (B50) Listen and repeat.

Weak pronunciation	Strong pronunciation
It was fun.	It **wasn't** boring.
Was it fun?	Yes, it **was**.
Were you busy yesterday?	No, I **wasn't**.

B. PAIRS. Role-play the conversations.

1. **A:** Were your friends at the party?
   B: No, they weren't.
2. **A:** Were you home last night?
   B: Yes, I was.

GRAMMAR FOCUS

The simple past of irregular verbs

Affirmative statements
Brian **went** to Miami two months ago.
Brian **spent** the summer there.

Negative statements
He **didn't go** to New York.
He **didn't spend** the winter there.

Yes/No questions
Did Brian **go** to Miami?
Did Brian **spend** the summer there?

Affirmative answers
Yes, he **did**.
Yes, he **did**.

Negative answers
No, he **didn't**.
No, he **didn't**.

Information questions
When **did** Brian **go** to Miami?
Who **went** to Miami?

Short answers
Two months ago.
Brian.

Long answers
He **went** to Miami two months ago.
Brian **went** to Miami.

Some irregular verbs

come → **came**	have → **had**	go → **went**	take → **took**
do → **did**	get → **got**	spend → **spent**	tell → **told**

Discovering grammar

Look at the grammar chart. Circle the correct answers.

1. Irregular verbs (*add* / *do not add*) *-d* or *-ed* to the base form to form the simple past.
2. In simple past questions, use the helping verb (*do* / *did*) with the base form of a main verb.

Practicing grammar

8 Practice

Read Brian's e-mail. Circle all the verbs in the simple past. Include both affirmative and negative forms.

> Hey! How are you guys doing?
>
> I (arrived) home on Sunday. I was really tired that day, so I went to bed at 8:00 P.M. When I woke up at 1:00, I went straight to the bathroom and took a shower. Of course, I didn't know it was one in the morning! My mom and dad weren't up, so I knocked on their bedroom door to ask about breakfast. "At one in the morning?" Mom asked.
>
> I'm glad I spent my summer with your family. Your dad's job as a computer animator is so cool! I think I'm going to study computer technology.
>
> My parents said hi. Thanks again for a great summer.
>
> I miss you all.
>
> Brian

9 Practice

Write two sentences to correct the information.

1. Brian went to Canada as an exchange student.
   Brian didn't go to Canada.
   He went to the United
   States.

2. He came back to Australia last month.
   _____
   _____

3. On Sunday, he went to bed at 10 P.M.
   _____
   _____

4. He took a shower at 6 A.M.
   _____
   _____

5. Brian spent the summer with his grandparents.
   _____
   _____

10 Practice

Have a competition! Go to page 133.

11 Writing

A. GROUPS. Write a story using the simple past. Follow the instructions.

1. Read the two beginning sentences. Write one of these sentences on a piece of paper. *It was a dark and rainy night.* OR *It was a bright and sunny day.*

2. The first student adds a second sentence to the story and passes the paper on to the next student who then writes in the third sentence. (The sentences can be funny or ridiculous.)

3. Continue until all students in the group have contributed a sentence. The last student to get the paper should end the story.

B. GROUPS. Read your stories out loud to the class.

12 Communication

Talk about past activities

A. B51 Listen to the conversation.

> **A:** Did you do anything fun last week?
> **B:** Yes, I did! We went to the amusement park.
> **A:** What did you do there?
> **B:** My little brother and I tried the new ride at the park. It was so scary!
> **A:** Did your brother scream?
> **B:** No, he didn't. But I did.

B. PAIRS. Role-play the conversation or make up your own about a past weekend activity.

13 Vocabulary

Some occupations

A. B52 Look at the photos as you listen and repeat.

web designer driver hairdresser mechanic

nurse electrician dentist pilot carpenter doctor

B. Read the clues. Then complete the crossword puzzle.

ACROSS
3. operates aircraft
4. drives cars and trucks
5. makes things out of wood
6. treats sick people
8. assists doctors
9. creates websites (2 words)
10. fixes cars

DOWN
1. connects and repairs electrical equipment
2. cleans and treats people's teeth
7. cuts and styles hair

14 Listening

A. (B53) **Listen to the conversation. Circle the occupations you hear.**

a. carpenter   d. doctor   g. police officer

b. dentist   e. pilot   h. engineer

c. nurse   f. mechanic   i. actor

B. (B54) **Listen again. Circle the correct answers.**

1. "Teen Line's" topic for today is "Occupations for the (*21st / 22nd*) century."
2. Mario's dad is (*a car / an airplane*) mechanic.
3. Isabel's (*grandma / mom*) is a doctor.
4. Isabel wants to be a (*dentist / doctor*).
5. The boys on the show want to be (*police officers / firefighters*).

15 Reading

A. **Look up the meaning of the underlined words in the article.**

B. (B55) **Read along silently as you listen.**

GROUPS. Talk about your favorite occupations. Ask each other questions about them.

Useful language:
- What occupations do you like?
- Why do you like it/them?
- Which would you like to be when you grow up?
- Yeah, that's a cool job.
- Me, too./I like it, too.
- Maybe.

Hot jobs for the 21st century

When your parents were very young, they probably wanted to be a doctor or a lawyer or an engineer when they grew up. Those were the hot jobs many years ago. But what will the hot jobs be when you grow up?

Science and technology continue to change how we live. When you grow up, there will be new occupations that we don't have today. Here are some futuristic occupations from Time.com's "Visions of the Century":

1. Hotline handymen (repairmen/technicians): Are your parents afraid to program their VCRs and DVD players? What will they do when 3-D televisions and talking toasters become a reality? *You*, however, do not need to worry. In the future, technicians will be able to take care of your <u>appliance</u> problems from their computers, without going to your home.

2. Virtual-reality actors: Do you request pay-per-view movies on your TV? In pay-per-view, you pay to watch a movie. In the future, pay-per-view will become pay-per-play. In pay-per-play, you will pay to be a part of the movie you're watching. You won't just watch the actors in a movie. You will be able to interact with them. For example, you can tell Tom Cruise to look out when there's <u>danger</u>! That would be really awesome!

16 Comprehension

Discuss and answer these questions.

According to the article, . . .

1. What were some of the popular occupations during your parents' time?
2. What do hotline handymen do?
3. What can you do with virtual-reality actors?

17 Speaking

GROUPS. Discuss these questions.

1. What other futuristic occupations would you like to have? Discuss two.
2. What two inventions or products would you like to see in the future? Describe what these inventions can do.

> **Test-taking tip:** Review your answers.
> After answering all the questions, review your answers. Correct any errors.

Grammar

**A. Write the past forms of the verbs.
(1 point each)**

1. is/am ___was___
2. are _____
3. shop _____
4. take _____
5. make _____
6. do _____
7. try _____
8. tell _____
9. go _____
10. come _____

**B. Complete the sentences with the simple past form of the verbs in parentheses.
(1 point each)**

1. My friend Sherri and I (be) ___were___ at a rock concert last Saturday.
2. We (see) _____ some of our classmates there.
3. We (call) _____ their names.
4. But they (not/hear) _____ us.
5. The concert (be) _____ awesome.
6. We (have) _____ a lot of fun.

C. Change sentences 2, 3, 4, and 6 in Exercise B into *Yes/No* questions. Then answer them. (3 points each sentence)

1. Q: _Did we see our classmates at the_ _concert?_
   A: _Yes, we did._
2. Q: _____
   A: _____
3. Q: _____
   A: _____
4. Q: _____
   A: _____

D. Write information questions about the underlined parts in the sentences. Use the cues. (2 points each)

1. Brian spent his summer <u>in the U.S.</u>
   (Where) _Where did Brian spend his_ _summer?_

2. He went back to Australia <u>last month</u>.
   (When) _____
3. He was in the U.S. <u>because he was an exchange student</u>.
   (Why) _____
4. He invited <u>his parents</u> to visit him.
   (Who) _____

Vocabulary

**E. Write the occupation for each definition.
(1 point each)**

1. operates aircraft ___pilot___
2. drives buses and trucks _____
3. creates websites _____
4. cuts and styles hair _____
5. treats people's teeth _____

Communication

F. Talk about what you did on your last birthday. Ask *Yes/No* and information questions. Use the cues. (2 points each sentence)

A: (Yes/No *question*)
   Did you have a party?
B: _Yes, I had a party with my friends._
A: (*Information question*)
   _____
B: _____
A: (Yes/No *question*)
   _____
B: _____

> **Now I can . . .**
> ❏ talk about past events.
> ❏ express approval and disapproval.
> ❏ talk about occupations.

WORKING TEEN$

Many teens in the United States have part-time jobs, especially during summer vacation. They make new friends, earn money, and learn about the world of work.

I work in a fast-food restaurant. I started last summer. All my friends had summer jobs, and I was bored because I had nothing to do. So I interviewed here and got the job. The manager liked my work, and asked me to work for him again this summer. I've made some good friends here, and it's fun earning my own money. I'm saving up to buy my first car. I'm so sick of asking my parents, "Can I borrow the keys?"

Maria Martinez, 16

Some of my friends still get allowances from their parents, but I work for my spending money. During the school year, I babysit on weekends. I charge $7 an hour. I also take care of dogs and cats at my home when the owners are away. I earn $25 a day. My mom helps with that. In the spring and summer, I also do yard work. I charge $10 an hour. And I wash cars, too—I charge $15 a car. Washing cars is tiring, but it pays well. I get most of my work from word-of-mouth, but I also put up posters around the neighborhood.

Jane Weston, 13

Common Teen Jobs

babysitting

washing cars

helping children with homework

pet sitting

working at a restaurant

being a lifeguard at a pool

dog walking

working in a store

working at a summer camp

doing yard work

being a coach

1 Reading

> **Reading skill:** Guessing word meaning from context
> When you read, try to guess the meanings of new words.
> Look for clues in the text and pictures.

A. Read the article and look at the pictures. Then draw lines from the vocabulary items to their meanings.

1.	fast food	a.	people talking about it
2.	earn money	b.	sports instructor
3.	coach	c.	burgers, French fries, etc.
4.	pays well	d.	money parents give children
5.	allowance	e.	make money by working
6.	word-of-mouth	f.	gives you a lot of money

B. Read the article again. Write short answers to the questions.

1. Why was Maria bored? _____

2. What does Brandon want to be? _____

3. How many different jobs does Jane do? _____

2 Listening

B56 **Listen to Amy tell her friend about her summer job. Write short answers to the questions.**

1. What job did Amy do? _____

2. Why did she want to do it? _____

3. What was bad about the job? _____

4. What is Amy saving up for? _____

3 Speaking

PAIRS. Give your opinions of the American teen jobs listed in the box. Use these words and phrases.

easy	interesting	exciting	good experience	pays well
difficult	boring	tiring	dangerous	doesn't pay well

4 Writing

Think of a job for next summer and write a paragraph about it. Answer these questions:

- Why is it a good job for you?
- What's good about it? What's bad about it?
- What do you want to do with the money?

I'm a tennis coach at a summer camp for physically challenged elementary school children. It's my first job and it's been great. I love tennis and I love coaching. In fact, I plan to be a professional coach in the future. So this job is giving me some very good experience. I have about fifty students, and I really make them work!

Brandon Parker, 15

Fun with songs 1

A *list of our favorite songs*

A. **GROUPS.** On a piece of paper, make two columns with the heads *Favorite English songs* and *Favorite local songs*.

B. **GROUPS.** Talk about your favorite songs. Choose two to three songs for each column. List their titles and the names of the singers. Use the Useful language in your discussion.

C. **GROUPS.** Present your list to the class. Write the song titles and the singers' names on the board.

D. **CLASS.** Look at the titles on the board. Vote on your top three favorite songs in each category. Copy the titles of the top songs in your notebook.

E. *Homework*: Listen to as many of the songs on the class list as you can. Which songs do you like best? Why?

F. **CLASS.** Share your reactions to the songs with your classmates.

Useful language:
- What's your favorite local song?
- It's/He/She's/They're my favorite, too.
- Me, too.
- What about English songs?
- Yeah, that's a really cool song.
- Who's the singer?
- How about you? What's your favorite?

Fun with songs 2

A favorite song chorus

And I think you feel that way, too.

Please, please, please don't go!

I'm so happy when I'm with you.

Because I love you so.

I can't live without you.

Materials:
- Enlarged copies of the chorus of a favorite song, cut up into separate lines
- Recording of the song

A. **CLASS.** Form teams. Your teacher will give you cut-up lines from a favorite song. Your task is to put the lines together to form the chorus as fast as you can.

B. **GROUPS.** Form teams. Read the lines carefully and discuss their meaning. Use a dictionary if helpful. Discuss how to put the lines together. Use the Useful language in your discussion.

C. **GROUPS.** Write the completed chorus on a piece of paper. Raise your hands once you're finished.

D. **GROUPS.** Your teacher will play a recording of the song. Check your work as you listen.

E. **CLASS.** Share your experience. Talk about these points:
- What is the chorus about?
- What words helped you put the chorus together?
- Was the task easy or difficult? Did you enjoy it?

Useful language:
- Let's read all the lines first.
- What does . . . mean?
- I think this line comes first/next/last.
- No, this is first/next/last.
- It still isn't right.
- I think that's it!

Fun with songs 3

A poster of a favorite singer or band

Materials:

- Poster board
- Markers or crayons
- Pictures of a favorite singer or group
- Recording of a favorite song

A. GROUPS. Choose a favorite singer or band, either local or international. Use the Useful language in your discussion. Choose a song to play during your presentation.

B. *Homework*: Research the singer or band. Find out where they're from, their real names, the titles of their hit songs, and any other fun facts about them. Find pictures of them in magazines or on the Internet. Bring your notes, pictures, and a recording of the song to class.

C. GROUPS. Create a poster featuring your favorite singer or group. Include the information and photos you found during your research.

D. GROUPS. Present your poster to the class. Give facts about the singer or band and play their song for the class. Ask your classmates for their comments and questions.

Useful language:

- Who's your favorite singer or band?
- He/She/They sing(s) the song . . .
- What's their best song?
- How about . . . ?
- I really like him/her/them/it, too.
- I don't like him/her/them/it that much.
- Let's choose . . . as our favorite.

Fun with songs 4

A collage about a favorite song

Materials:

- Poster board
- Markers or crayons
- Recording and lyrics of a favorite song
- Pictures illustrating the lyrics

A. GROUPS. Choose a favorite song, either local or international.

B. *Homework*:
- Find the lyrics to the song you chose in Step A. Listen to the song and read the lyrics. What is the song about?
- Find pictures that illustrate the lyrics.
- Bring the lyrics, your notes, your pictures, and a recording of the song to class.

C. GROUPS. Discuss what the song is about and the images the lyrics suggest. Use the Useful language in your discussion.

D. GROUPS. Make a collage about the song. Include the song's title, the singer or band, and pictures illustrating the lyrics.

E. GROUPS. Present your collage to the class.
- Talk about the song you're going to play. Tell the class what it is about.
- Explain the pictures in the collage.
- Play the song.
- Ask your classmates for their comments and questions.

Useful language:

- This song is about a girl/a boy/a couple.
- They're on a beach/in the city.
- It's early morning/late at night.
- He's very happy/lonely/angry.
- They like/love/hate/can't stand each other.
- She wants a boyfriend/a new life.
- It's a very romantic/happy/sad/ song.

Focus on culture 1

All about Australia

My country, Australia, is the only country that's a continent. It's in the Southern Hemisphere. It's a beautiful country with many things to see and do.

Most Australians live in towns and cities near the ocean. Sydney is the largest city in Australia. It's on the east coast, and it's almost always sunny and warm. Sydney Harbor is beautiful.

The Great Barrier Reef is also on the east coast. It's the largest reef in the world. You can see lots of cool fish. But watch out for the sharks!

The middle of the country, the Outback, is hot and dry. Not many people live there. But there are some cool places to see. Many people visit the Outback to see Uluru, a huge rock in the desert. It's 345 meters tall and 3 kilometers wide!

Australia has lots of unusual animals. One animal we're famous for is the kangaroo. There are over 40 different kinds of kangaroos. Kangaroos hop very quickly on their strong legs, and they carry their babies in a pouch.

Another unusual animal we have is the Tasmanian Devil. It lives in Tasmania, an island that's part of Australia. The Tasmanian Devil has very sharp teeth and a strange, loud scream. It hunts at night, and eats almost any animal it can find.

1 Comprehension

A. Identify each numbered photo. Choose from the box below.

| Uluru | Sydney Harbor | kangaroos |
| Tasmanian devil | the Great Barrier Reef | |

1. _Uluru_
2. _____
3. _____
4. _____
5. _____

B. Write *True* or *False* for each statement.

1. ___False___ Australia is the only country that's an island.
2. _____ The largest reef in the world is on Australia's east coast.
3. _____ Most people in Australia live in the middle of the country.
4. _____ Uluru is in the hot, dry Outback.
5. _____ The Tasmanian devil looks for food at night.

2 Comparing cultures

GROUPS. Discuss the questions below. Share the results with the class.

1. Is your country in the Northern or Southern Hemisphere?
2. Where do most people live in your country?
3. What's the largest city in your country?
4. What are some famous places in your country?
5. What are some famous animals in your country?

3 Your turn

PAIRS. Write a paragraph about one of the topics below. Share your paragraph with your classmates.

1. Facts about your country
2. Interesting places to visit in your country
3. Interesting animals in your country

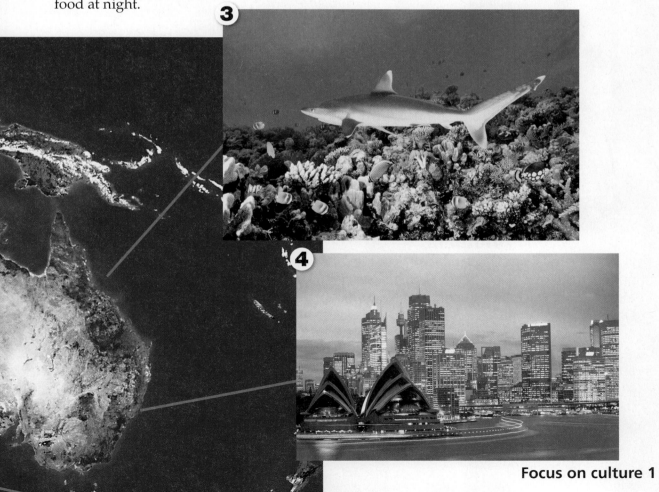

Birthdays around the World

Japan

As in many other countries, Japanese kids eat cake and open presents on their birthdays. And for young children, there is a special celebration in February called the "3-5-7 Festival." This is for boys aged 3 and 5, and girls aged 3 and 7. Children wear traditional clothes on this day. They eat special sweets called "thousand-year candies" so they will live a long life. The twentieth birthday is also important in Japan. This is when Japanese teenagers become adults. Each city has a special event for all 20-year-olds in January.

Mexico

At birthday parties in Mexico, kids break piñatas. Piñatas are made of paper and have candy and fruit inside. The birthday boy or girl puts on a blindfold and tries to hit the piñata with a stick. When the piñata breaks, the other kids run to pick up the candy. On their fifteenth birthday, Mexican girls are called "Quinceañeras." They have a big, expensive party with dinner, music, and dancing. The birthday girl wears a beautiful dress and jewelry. She dances first with different young men, then with her father and other relatives.

Vietnam

In Vietnam, everybody celebrates his or her birthday on the same day—New Year's Day. It doesn't matter what day you were born. On New Year's Day, everyone is one year older. Everyone wears new clothes, and there are fireworks and parades. Young people get red envelopes from their parents and other adults. Inside the envelopes is "lucky money." At the end of the day, young people open the envelopes and count their money!

1 Comprehension

A. What does each photo show? Write the letter of the photo next to each description.

1. ___E___ Japan: cake and presents
2. _____ Japan: the 3-5-7 Festival
3. _____ Mexico: piñata
4. _____ Mexico: Quinceañeras
5. _____ Vietnam: fireworks
6. _____ Vietnam: red envelope

B. Write short answers for each question.

1. What do kids in Japan eat for the "3-5-7 Festival"? _____

2. At what age do Japanese become adults? _____

3. How do kids break piñatas in Mexico? _____

4. At what age do Mexican girls have expensive parties? _____

5. When do people in Vietnam celebrate their birthdays? _____

6. What do people in Vietnam wear on that day? _____

7. What do young people get in red envelopes? _____

2 Comparing cultures

GROUPS. Discuss these questions.

1. What do you do on birthdays in your country?
2. What does the birthday boy or girl wear?
3. Who gives presents?
4. What kind of presents do people give?
5. What else do people do on birthdays?
6. Do boys and girls have a special party at a certain age?
7. When do people become adults?

3 Your turn

Write a paragraph about birthdays in your country.

Focus on culture 3

Amusement Parks around the World

Universal Studios and Islands of Adventure, U.S.A.

You can see how movies are made at Florida's Universal Studios and Islands of Adventure. And even more fun, you can ride thrill rides based on hit movies. Revenge of the Mummy, for example, is a scary indoor roller coaster. Mummies jump out as you speed through the dark. On the Jurassic Park River Adventure, there are hungry dinosaurs all around you. Or try the Incredible Hulk Coaster, a huge high-speed green roller coaster. You go from 0 to 60 kilometers per hour in two seconds, and the coaster turns you upside down seven times!

Port Aventura, Spain

At Spain's Port Aventura, you can "visit" Mexico, China, Polynesia, the Mediterranean, and America's Far West. You can eat food, buy gifts, and see sights from each of these places. The Far West is especially cool—it's an old cowboy town from the 1800s. And there are some fantastic rides! In Mexico, you can ride the Hurakan Condor. It takes you 100 meters up in the air, then drops you. In China, you can ride the Dragon Khan—it's the only roller coaster in the world with eight full loops.

Futuroscope, France

Visit France's Futuroscope amusement park to see the future. In the Robot Zoo, you can see and touch giant robotic animals and insects. In Travelers by Sea and Air, you sit in a movie theater of the future. There is one screen in front of you and one under your feet. You feel like you're deep in the sea or high in the air. Or you can ride on one of the ten 7-meter-high dancing robot arms of Dances with Robots. The robots dance to techno music in a robot disco. As they dance, they turn you in all directions. And when you're hungry, you can eat at le Cristal. This restaurant serves food of the future made by a famous French chef.

④

1 Comprehension

A. Write the letter of each amusement park next to its description below.

   a. Universal Studios and Islands of Adventure
   b. Port Aventura
   c. Futuroscope

   1. _____ You can feel like you're visiting the future.

   2. _____ You can imagine you're in different countries.

   3. _____ You can see mummies and dinosaurs from hit movies.

B. What does each photo show? Write the number of the photo next to the name of the attraction in the box below.

⑤

>   _6_ **Dances with Robots**
>   _____ **America's Far West**
>   _____ **Incredible Hulk Coaster**
>   _____ **Revenge of the Mummy**
>   _____ **Travelers by Sea and Air**
>   _____ **Jurassic Park River Adventure**

2 Comparing cultures

GROUPS. Discuss these questions.

1. What are some fun amusement parks in your country?
2. Where are they?
3. What are some cool rides there?
4. What is each ride like?

3 Your turn

Write a paragraph about an amusement park in your country.

⑥

Focus on culture 4

Teens' Rooms around the U.S.

In the United States, a teenager's room is usually very important to him or her. Some teens share a room with a brother or sister, but most have their own space. You can learn a lot about American teens by looking at their rooms.

Judy, Los Angeles

My room is very personal to me. It's my space, and my parents can't come in. My room is my work of art, my diary, and my scrapbook. My walls are dark orange—my favorite color. I don't write things down in a diary. Instead, I write my thoughts and ideas on my walls. That way I can look at them and think about them anytime. I also put other things I like on my walls—notes from friends, photos, tickets, pages from magazines, whatever. Do you want to know the real me? Just look at my room.

Lauren, New York City

I spend a lot of time in my room. I talk to friends on my cell, surf the Internet, do homework, read, and just relax. My room is long and narrow, but it's pretty big—at least for New York. I have a computer desk, bookshelves, and a four-poster bed. On my walls I have posters, photos of friends, and a big red heart. My best friend gave me the heart for my birthday. I also have blue curtains, a hot pink chair, and a green hanging basket. I like bright colors. My mom says my room is messy. But I like to have my clothes and things scattered around. That way I can find things easily!

Terry, Chicago

My room is my studio. I play my keyboards and practice for gigs there. I'm in a hip-hop band called Box, and we sometimes play in my garage. My room is above the garage, away from the other rooms in the house. So I can be pretty loud in my room. That's my favorite thing about it. I don't have a lot of stuff. I just have an old bunk bed, a dresser, my keyboard, and speakers. I guess I like things simple. I sleep and play music in my room, and that's about it.

3

1 Comprehension

A. Whose room is it? Write the number of the photo next to each name.

Judy _____   Lauren _____   Terry _____

B. Write short answers to the questions below.

1. Why does Lauren have blue curtains and a hot pink chair? _Because she likes bright_ _colors._

2. Why does Lauren like her clothes and things scattered around? _____
_____

3. What is Terry's favorite thing about his room? _____
_____

4. Why doesn't Terry have a lot of stuff? _____
_____

5. Why does Judy write her thoughts and ideas on her walls? _____
_____

6. How is Judy's room her "scrapbook"? _____
_____

2 Comparing cultures

PAIRS. Discuss these questions.

1. Is your room important to you? Why/Why not?
2. Do you spend much time in your room? Why/Why not?
3. What furniture do you have?
4. What do you have on your walls? Why?
5. What else is special about your room? Why?

3 Your turn

Write a paragraph about your own room. Explain what it shows about you.

Fun with grammar

Unit 1, 11 Practice, page 10

For the student: Form two lines, line A and line B. The lines should face each other so that every student is standing across from a student in the other line.

Line A:	S1	S2	S3	S4	S5	S6	S7	S8
Line B:	S1	S2	S3	S4	S5	S6	S7	S8

Take turns asking and answering the three questions from the grammar chart: *What's your name? How old are you? Who's your favorite singer?* (All pairs will be speaking at the same time, so it will be very noisy in the room!) After both students in each pair have asked the questions, everyone in line A should move down one. The student at the beginning of Line A moves to the other end of his or her line.

Line A:	S2	S3	S4	S5	S6	S7	S8	S1
Line B:	S1	S2	S3	S4	S5	S6	S7	S8

Ask and answer the three questions again with your new partner. Then line A moves down one again. Continue this pattern, each time trying to ask and answer the questions more quickly. Stop when students are back in their original positions.

Unit 2, 9 Practice, page 17

For the teacher: First, choose two students to help you monitor the class. Make sure everyone has the objects named below. Say the instructions. Students are out of the game if they do the action incorrectly.

1. Put your English book **under** your desk.
2. Put it **in** your backpack.
3. Hold it **above** your head.
4. Put it **on** the floor.
5. Put it **in front of** your chair.
6. Put it **behind** your chair.
7. Put it **on** your desk.
8. Put your pen **in front of** your English book.
9. Put your pen **on** your notebook.

Unit 3, 7 Practice, page 27

For the student: Write the plural form of each noun in one minute. The student who gets the most correct answers wins.

Singular	Plural
actress	_____
person	_____
key	_____
glass	_____
pencil	_____
baby	_____
fox	_____
place	_____
tooth	_____
child	_____
man	_____
chair	_____
berry	_____
mouse	_____
tooth	_____

Unit 4, 10 Practice, page 37

For the teacher: Make sure that the students are seated in rows. Each row is a team. Assign ordinal numbers for each row; for example, row 1 is the first row.

Have the students in each row count off, each row beginning with number 1. Give a command to a student from any row, using ordinals to identify the student.

For example: The sixth student in the first row, raise your hand. If the student responds quickly and correctly, he or she earns a point for the team.

Unit 5, 11 Practice, page 45

For the teacher: Form two teams. Draw a tic-tac-toe grid on the board. Explain how to play. You will say something about Rufus. Members of the two teams compete to correct your statement. The team that gives the correct answer runs to the board and fills in a box in the tic-tac-toe grid. Use these statements.

1. Rufus has four sisters.
   (Rufus doesn't have four sisters. He has four brothers.)
2. Mr. and Mrs. Garcia have four cats.
3. The cats have blue eyes.
4. Mr. and Mrs. Garcia have a small house.
5. The house has a backyard.
6. The house has six bedrooms.
7. Rufus has a big bed.
8. Rufus has a difficult life.

Unit 6, 14 Practice, page 56

For the teacher: Tell the students to form a circle. Say a sentence, making one up or choosing from the list below. Make a humming sound for the missing word. Go around the circle and randomly call on a student to give the correct object pronoun. If that student answers correctly, he or she remains standing. If not, the student sits down.

For example:

1. I like rock music.
   I listen to _____ every day.
2. Where are Rob and Julia?
   I can't see _____.
3. My father is great.
   I love _____.
4. She loves hot dogs.
   She prefers _____ to hamburgers.
5. He doesn't like you and Paul.
   He can't stand _____.
6. Linda and I are Jackie's friends.
   Jackie likes _____.
7. The book is in the backpack.
   Kevin put _____ there.
8. I don't know him, but somehow
   he knows _____.

Unit 7, 6 Practice, page 64

For the teacher: Form groups of six. Choose one leader per group to give the following commands. The rest of the group must do the action at the same time. If someone is unable to perform the action, he or she must sit down. The last person standing is the leader for the next round of the game. This activity can also be done with the whole class. If done as a whole class, choose one or two students to go around and call out students who are unable to perform the action.

1. Stand up.
2. Stand on one foot.
3. Sit down.
4. Stand up.
5. Shake a classmate's hand.
6. Put your hands down.
7. Laugh.
8. Sing "Happy birthday."
9. Wave to your teacher.
10. Greet your teacher.

Unit 8, 10 Practice, page 74

For the teacher: You will need a very soft ball for tossing. Follow the instructions.

1. Tell students to stand up in a circle.
2. Ask a *How often* question and toss the ball to a student.
3. The student who catches the ball (that is, Student 1) answers the question in a complete sentence using an adverb of frequency.
   For example:
   Teacher: How often do you forget your English book at home?
   Student 1: I never forget my English book at home.
4. Student 1 then tosses the ball to a second student (that is, Student 2) and asks him or her a *How often* question. Student 2 answers the question. Repeat the process until all have had a chance to participate.

Unit 9, 4 Practice, page 81

For the teacher: Divide the class into two or more teams. Explain how to play the game. You will do the following: (1) choose a mystery word from Exercise 3 and (2) think of a sentence using the mystery word correctly, but (3) in place of the mystery word, say "yadda yadda." For example, "On weekends I often go with my family to the **yadda yadda**. We usually don't buy anything. We just walk around and go from store to store."

Assign a representative for each team. The team reps must raise their hands if they think they know the mystery word. The team rep who raises his/her hand first gets a chance to say the mystery word out loud. If the answer is wrong, another team gets the chance to steal the point. If all teams fail to give the correct word, create another sentence using the same word.

For example, "The yadda yadda in my town has lots of cool stores and really good restaurants." Continue using the same word in sentences until a team guesses the correct word (*mall*). For the next turn, assign a new representative for each team. Continue in this way as time allows.

Unit 10, 12 Practice, page 95

For the teacher: Prepare 12 strips of paper. On each strip, write an activity that can be easily acted out. Make sure students understand the words and phrases you use. Put the strips in a box. *For example*:

- eating melting ice cream
- eating very hot food
- watching a tennis or ping-pong match
- sitting behind a very tall person in a movie theater
- walking on a flooded street
- getting into very tight jeans
- taking a very cold shower
- holding a very hot object
- trying to call a taxi on a busy street
- standing in a crowded elevator

Form two teams. Alternately call on a student from each team to draw a strip of paper from the box. This student silently reads what's on the strip of paper and acts out the activity. His or her team gets first chance to guess what the student is doing. (For example, "You're eating ice cream.") If the team guesses incorrectly, the opposing team gets the chance to steal the point. Remind the teams that they should answer in complete sentences. No points will be given for incomplete sentences.

Unit 11, 5 Practice, page 100

For the teacher: Divide the class into teams A and B. Draw the two tic-tac-toe grids below on the board. Team A begins. A member of Team A calls out the past form of one of the verbs. If the team gives the correct form, it can put its mark (a circle or an *X*) on that verb in the tic-tac-toe grid. If the team gets it wrong, the other team can try to correct the mistake and steal the spot on the grid. Teams can use either grid, and they can move from one grid to another. The members of the teams take turns calling out the past forms of the verbs.

agree	avoid	call
clean	cry	decide
enjoy	stop	invite

organize	plan	smile
suggest	study	try
wait	wash	gossip

Unit 12, 10 Practice, page 112

For the teacher: Follow these instructions.

1. Divide the class into two teams. Give List A to Team A, List B to Team B. Tell students to try to memorize the simple past forms of the verbs. After three minutes, take the lists away.
2. On the board, make two lists of the base forms of some of the verbs. Each list should have the same verbs but arranged in a different order.
3. Have a representative from each team go to the board and choose any verb to write in the past.
4. Each student should write only one verb, but he or she may correct the previous student's answer. The first team to give all the correct answers wins.

List A			
1. am, is	**was**	7. tell	**told**
2. are	**were**	8. take	**took**
3. write	**wrote**	9. have	**had**
4. think	**thought**	10. go	**went**
5. come	**came**	11. spend	**spent**
6. do	**did**	12. get	**got**

List B			
1. get	**got**	7. go	**went**
2. do	**did**	8. are	**were**
3. have	**had**	9. tell	**told**
4. spend	**spent**	10. think	**thought**
5. write	**wrote**	11. come	**came**
6. am, is	**was**	12. take	**took**

Peer editing checklist

☐ **Is the first letter of each sentence capitalized?**

she is a student. ⟶ **She** is a student.

☐ **Are proper nouns (people's names, place names) capitalized?**

My brother's name is paul. ⟶ My brother's name is **Paul**.

He lives in los angeles. ⟶ He lives in **Los Angeles**.

☐ **Is there a period (.) or exclamation mark (!) at the end of each sentence?**

I like Shakira ⟶ I like Shakira**.**

She's cool ⟶ She's cool**!**

☐ **Is there a question mark (?) at the end of each question?**

What's your name ⟶ What's your name**?**

☐ **Is the vocabulary correct?**

My mother is fourteen. ⟶ My mother is **forty**.

☐ **Is the spelling correct?**

He's an excheng student. ⟶ He's an **exchange** student.

☐ **Do sentences and questions have the correct word order?**

You are a student? ⟶ **Are you** a student?

☐ **Are the verbs correct?**

I be fine. ⟶ I **am** fine.

He like hip-hop. ⟶ He **likes** hip-hop.

☐ **Are words such as *first*, *next*, or *after that* used if needed?**

I get up. I eat breakfast. ⟶ **First** I get up. **After that,** I eat breakfast.

☐ **Are the paragraphs clear and easy-to-understand?**

Her name is Anna. She likes sports. We play tennis. This is my sister. ⟶ This is my sister. Her name is Anna. She likes sports. She plays tennis. I do, too.

Word list

Let's get started.

baby, 4
beautiful, 4
big, 4
black, 2
blue, 2
board, 3
book, 3
boy, 4
brown, 2
crayons, 3
desk, 3
dime, 4
dollar, 4
door, 3
eraser, 3
floor, 3
folders, 3
girl, 4
green, 2
handsome, 4
man, 4
markers, 3
nickel, 4
notebook, 3
notepad, 3
old, 4
orange, 2
pair of scissors, 3
pen, 3
pencil, 3
penny, 4
poster board, 3
quarter, 4
red, 2
ruler, 3
short, 4
small, 4
student, 3
tall, 4
teacher, 3
teenager, 4
wall, 3
week, 2
weekend, 2
white, 2
window, 3
woman, 4
yellow, 2
young, 4

Unit 1

age, 6
airport, 13
author, 9
be (*am, is, are*), 8
city, 12

classmate, 8
excuse me, 7
favorite, 11
friend, 10
grade, 12
he, 8
homework, 8
I, 8
it, 8
movie, 12
movie director, 9
music, 12
name, 6
occupation, 9
province, 12
she, 8
singer, 9
sports, 12
state, 12
talk show host, 9
they, 8
town, 12
visitor, 6
we, 8
you, 8

Unit 2

above, 16
at, 16
backpack, 16
bag, 14
behind, 16
bicycle, 16
car, 14
cart, 14
cell phone, 16
computer, 16
DVD player, 16
family, 20
fun, 18
his, 18
her, 18
home, 14
in, 14
in front of, 14
kitchen, 17
leave alone, 14
like, 18
magazines, 16
MP3 player, 16
my, 18
new, 14
on, 14
over there, 14
phone, 17
our, 18
Rollerblades, 16

room, 14
show (*v.*), 14
skateboard, 16
table, 17
television, 16
their, 18
there, 14
video games, 14
where, 14
work, 14
your, 14

Unit 3

a/an, 28
activities, 30
American, 24
Australian, 24
awesome, 26
Brazilian, 24
British, 24
Canadian, 24
Chinese, 24
Colombian, 24
Costa Rican, 24
e-mail address, 25
exchange student, 26
Finnish, 24
Japanese, 24
know/learn by heart, 25
Korean, 24
Lebanese, 24
Mexican, 24
Moroccan, 24
nationality, 24
Polish, 24
skater, 26
that, 24
these, 24
this, 24
those, 24
tricks, 26
Venezuelan, 24

Unit 4

address, 34
baseball, 37
birthday, 37
date of birth, 34
digits, 34
event, 37
game, 37
guest pass, 34
first/last name, 34
of course, 34
oh, man!, 37
sorry, 34
spell, 34

trouble, 37
volleyball, 37
wait a minute, 37
what day, 34
what time, 34
when, 34
zip code, 34

Unit 5

aunt, 42
blond, 47
brother, 42
cousin, 42
curly, 47
father, 42
girlfriend, 44
grandfather, 42
grandmother, 42
grandparents, 42
hair, 44
has/have, 45
light brown, 47
long, 47
medium, 47
mother, 42
only child, 44
pictures, 44
pretty, 44
short, 47
sister, 42
straight, 47
uncle, 42
wallet, 44
wavy, 47

Unit 6

afford, 52
all kinds, 52
can't stand, 52
crazy about, 52
hate, 52
her, 56
him, 56
hip-hop, 52
into it, 52
loud, 52
love, 52
mad, 56
maybe, 52
me, 56
meet, 52
music, 52
prefer, 52
rap, 52
soon, 52
tomorrow, 56
us, 56

Word list

Unit 7

act, 66
borrow, 68
break dance, 67
can, 62
count, 65
dance, 66
draw, 66
drive, 66
erase, 68
help, 64
piano, 67
play soccer, 66
play the guitar, 66
ride a bike, 66
rude, 62
sing, 66
skateboard (v.), 66
speak, 66
swim, 66

Unit 8

alarm, 70
after that, 70
always, 70
banana, 70
brush teeth, 70
cereal, 70
check e-mail, 73
comb/brush hair, 72
do homework, 72
early, 73
eat or have breakfast, 70
eat or have dinner, 72
finally, 70
first, 70
get dressed, 70
get home from school, 72
get up, 70
go to bed, 72
go to school, 72
late, 70

never, 70
next, 70
nothing much, 73
often, 70
rarely, 73
seldom, 73
sleep, 74
sometimes, 70
start, 71
take a shower, 70
then, 70
usually, 70
wake up, 70
watch TV, 72

Unit 9

across from, 80
any, 80
bank, 81
beaches, 80
behind, 80
between, 80
bookstore, 81
bus stop, 81
dance club, 80
dolphins, 82
drugstore, 81
eat out, 86
go shopping, 86
go to a party, 86
go to the movies, 86
hang out, 80
have a party, 86
mall, 81
movie theater, 81
museum, 80
next to, 80
on the corner of, 80
paradise, 80
park, 80
place, 80
pool, 80

post office, 81
restaurant, 80
some, 80
supermarket, 81
there is/are, 80
visit, 80
watch a DVD, 86
waterfalls, 82
zoo, 80

Unit 10

bathroom, 91
bathroom scale, 96
bedroom, 90
bored, 95
bothering, 90
dining room, 91
downstairs, 90
garage, 91
grumpy, 90
kitchen, 91
living room, 91
not really, 95
oven, 96
refrigerator, 96
stairs, 91
upstairs, 90

Unit 11

a few minutes ago, 98
a month ago, 99
a week ago, 99
a year ago, 9
agree, 100
cake, 101
costume party, 98
decide, 100
gossip, 98
invite, 98
last Monday, 99
last month, 99
last night, 99

last week, 99
last year, 99
lemonade, 101
stop, 100
stop by, 98
suggest, 98
surprise party, 98
three days ago, 99
want, 98
yesterday, 98

Unit 12

actor, 114
animator, 112
appliance, 114
carpenter, 113
cyberspace, 114
dentist, 113
doctor, 113
driver, 113
dude, 108
electrician, 113
engineer, 114
glad, 108
hairdresser, 113
handymen, 114
house call, 114
illness, 114
mechanic, 113
nun, 110
nurse, 113
painter, 110
pilot, 113
police officer, 114
repairmen, 114
scientist, 110
sheep, 114
technician, 114
vaccine, 114
virtual reality, 114
web designer, 114